AN INQUIRY

To What End?

AN INQUIRY

To What End?

CHRISTIE HARDWICK

Park Point
PRESS

Park Point Press is an imprint of Centers for Spiritual Living
573 Park Point Drive | Golden CO 80401

Park Point Press
An imprint of Centers for Spiritual Living
573 Park Point Drive
Golden, CO 80401-7402
720-496-1370
www.csl.org/publications/books

Printed in the United States of America
Publication Date: December 2024

Editor: Julie Mierau
Design/Layout: Maria Robinson, Designs On You, LLC

ISBN paperback: 978-1-956198-48-5
ISBN ebook: 978-1-956198-49-2

Dedicated to my children

by birth and marriage

who invite me to greater love every day—

Joshua, Victoria, Matteo and Max.

I woke up in the middle of the night wondering:

To what end am I living?

To love deep or to love wide?

Can I achieve both?

Table of Contents

Foreword

Love is everywhere, weaving through everything, deep and abundant, expansive and overflowing. We are immersed in its ocean. Love has and will always have a limitless quality and enduring truth that guides human nature.

Love beckons from within all experiences, calling for us to see the wholeness and beauty that is our true essence. Love invites us to the highest vantage point, where we look beyond ego identities. It is here that we hold the vigil and vision of the infinite beauty and essence of ourselves, all others, and this world.

Love undergirds all things, including what's seemingly cloaked in darkness, falling apart, or broken. It holds us in the challenges, leaps of faith, heartbreaks, fumbling, and stumbling. When peering with a softened eye and tender heart, love and light reveal themselves amidst the crevices, cracks, bruises, and wounds of life. Love knows how capable we are and assists us in that rise, unconditionally.

We each are human starlight, come to illuminate the darkness. When things flow well, our rays of light and love may be unseen, because light is not often noticeable within light. Christie Hardwick provides a beautiful map of how we can become more intimate with ourselves and the world. She weaves a sacred cloth, first in the personal vignettes shared in her first book, *Radical Self-Tenderness,* and now in one, *To What End?*. These intimate threads weave together the simplicity, beauty, and innocence of the human life we wear.

In this book, Christie poses a powerful question, one that pushes against the edges of identity and our current areas of focus, action, and intention. She writes: "To what end am I living? To feel peace rather than agitation. To love well... ." This book represents a voyage, an adventure into the great mystery of who we are and why we are here, by way of her example.

When we open to the power of inquiry, introspection, and listening that follows her lead, the insights and wisdom are worth keeping alive. Being seen and heard empowers us to continually open our hearts. They empower our individual and collective humanity. When grounded in that core, we have the strength to be fully who we are. Such inquiry supports each one of us in offering our unique soul elixir to the world. Walking into our valleys and up to places within that are the most high, we are more able to objectively look across our inner and outer life topographies—and awaken our most tender aspects.

As a mentor, guide, author, and teacher, I unceasingly advocate that our greatest service lies in doing our inner work consistently, continually engaging in deep practice and steady alignment. You may question this approach at times, wondering why can't we skip all this and just get to enlightenment already. But, it is our sweet self-discovery that our souls yearn for. Our souls, and our Source, want to express through each of us and bear sacred witness to how our spiritual buds blossom.

The divine energies within call us to our healing power and wholeness, inviting us to heal our ways, ourselves, each other, and our Earth. Our divine energy calls us to embrace radical self-tenderness. Our divine energy is the part of us that asks, with Christie, "To what end?", and awaits the inspired action that will initiate a new and higher way in the world.

This life is for living, being, and knowing yourself. Unlock your meaningful life. To that end, live well, love well, and, with Spirit, be used well.

~ SIMRAN SINGH

Author of the self-realization trilogy of
Living, Being, and Knowing
Publisher of 11:11 Magazine & Host of 11:11 Talk Radio

Prologue

I have a privileged, adventurous, and abundant life. I am a Black American, and in spite of its flaws, my country allowed me to prosper. I accomplished a lot by any standard, and I give of myself in numerous ways. Yet I wonder, to what end am I living? I hope to live for a few more decades, but, of course, there is no guarantee. So I want to give my best to life today.

I want to love better and deeper. I wonder, would it be sufficient to do so in my own little constellation, or do I need to learn to love more of the world? Is love enough of a purpose, or do I need to accomplish great things?

This book is my attempt to answer these questions for myself. May something here stir your heart to your questions and your answers. And may you love well.

AN INQUIRY

To What End?

Living with the Question

chapter 1

Be patient toward all that is unsolved in your heart, and try to love the questions themselves as if they were locked rooms or books written in a very foreign language.

~ Rainer Maria Rilke

When I woke up with the question repeatedly in my mind, I felt peace rather than agitation, which intrigued me. To what end am I living? I took a deep breath and felt my body rise and fall. I stretched and stroked my thighs, sore from walking along the river. The answer came as simply this: to love well. And immediately another question: To love well means deep and wide? Or to love well means you and your beloved exploding in love for each other?

In my drifting, semi-dreaming state, I imagined loving the woman lying next to me deeply enough to send out a vibration as powerful as a supernova. Even though it feels overly dramatic, I feel compelled to continue the analogy.

One of my bucket list items is to see the northern lights, the aurora borealis. I want to stand before the sky and feel its immensity and my insignificance simultaneously. What am I in the face of the magnificence of the heavens, the unlimited nature of universes? And what do my few moments on the planet need to mean?

To what end, I wonder. When I leave this planet, what will I have accomplished? Does it matter at all what I do? Won't the Earth continue to turn and rotate around the sun, and people will be born and die? People will be kind and mean and happy and angry. People will make things, break things, and throw things away. Animals will thrive, or animals will die. The seas will survive, or the waters will suffer from our human mindlessness. The air will be clean or dirty, breathable or toxic. And what will my contribution be?

I have told myself that everything I think, say, and do matters to the whole. And I have come to understand that there's something immutable, unlimited, and ever-present that will not be affected by what I think, say, and do. I will either be a catalyst for that "something" or a constraint to its free-flowing through me.

I once wrote a song with these lyrics: "I know I'm one with the stars, the moon, the sky. One with the rainbow and every cloud passing by... ." This line came from reading an article in *Science* magazine that explained how all matter is made of the same elements. I found it crazy to think that if you reconfigure the DNA of a pig, you get a human. If you break down the elements in the earth, you find them in our bodies. There is an underlying unity that both intrigues and mystifies. If I am one with everything else and made of the same stuff, how do I live and breathe and have my being as part of a unified whole?

I try to love all these questions, as writer Rainer Marie Rilke suggests. If I can love these questions, I can unlock the freedom

to live like I have never lived before. Loving the question—
To what end?—is a key to unlocking a meaningful life. But
how to begin to explore this question? It starts with describing life as it is, without the answer.

A Day-By-Day Exploration

Some days, I am crystal clear about my purpose on the planet.
I wake up intending to do no harm to myself or others and
to do some good. When I remember to kiss my wife in the
morning and to tell her something lovely, this is a worthwhile
day. If I manage to give loving or kind attention to someone
else, this is a bonus.

On other days—sadly, most days—I'm not as clear. It isn't
enough to be loving or kind to my wife and others. I expect
to accomplish things.

I give myself credit for baking something healthy for us.
I judge myself worthy by walking the prescribed number of
steps. I count it as contributing to the world when I say
something positive and send it out via one of the platforms
we've created to talk with each other. If I do all these things,
I end the day feeling like I was good. I give myself a good
grade, but it doesn't last more than the time it takes me to
go to sleep.

When I've had a deeply enjoyable day, full of sights and tastes
and pleasing sounds, I celebrate. I think this also a worthwhile day. Enjoying my life is a good thing. And then come the
thoughts about places where suffering seems unrelenting.

And, of course, if I put my attention on it, I can find suffering absolutely everywhere I look. These days, I don't have to look. I can sit quietly and think about others in the world, and their pain arises in my mind.

Thinking about the suffering happening elsewhere can stop me in my tracks. I used to spend a lot of time tamping down my own good because it felt bad in contrast to all the suffering. But I do this less now. I recognize that my suffering on behalf of people does not benefit them or relieve their suffering, It just adds one more person to the mix.

If I think being good, rather than suffering, is what I am here to do, I need to know empirically what being good looks like. Being good is a moving target. What I thought I needed to do to be worthy, to be good, continues to change.

The Moving Target

chapter 2

When I was growing up, all I cared about was staying out of trouble and getting reinforcing strokes. I found joy in a few things, from the age of awareness until I was ten or so. My elementary school gave students certificates printed on crinkly rice paper. Depending on the achievement, the color of the certificate's border would be different. Orange, yellow, blue, purple, and green—I collected them all and loved to take them out and touch them regularly. They said I was good about attendance, about finishing assignments, about getting good grades, about being a good citizen, and about being consistent in all these accomplishments.

The targets in grade school were the grade, the teacher's attention, and the rub on the head I might get at home.

Another childhood target aimed at collecting enough money to go to the liquor store at the end of our unpaved street to buy candy and soda. I was addicted to sugar early on. While I could be found with redwood stains on my knees from climbing a fence to steal peaches, you'd more likely see me walking down the street with a paper bag full of licorice whips and a can of Cactus Cooler. Having candy felt like winning a prize, and when I consumed it, I felt all was right with the world.

You can imagine how I loved Halloween. Back in the late 1960s and early 1970s in our northern California suburbs, we were safe to wander for miles, collecting treats in pillowcases. My mother sorted my pillowcase bounty, throwing out anything she decided looked "suspicious" and gave me the rest. I would lovingly sort by color and type, saving my favorites in a separate pile to be hidden. With great reverence, I stacked the mini Almond Joys, Sugar Babies, Black Cows, and Reese's Peanut Butter Cups for the pleasure they would bring. My stash would last almost until Christmas. Candy was its own reward.

Sugar, candy, sweets of all kinds remained a pleasurable reward for most of my life. I took a few breaks, cleaned up, ate less of it, but I didn't really give up the addiction until my sixtieth year.

Forging My Identity

In my second decade of life, I started to desire being heard, seen, and given recognition. The sweets and written rewards were not enough, once I noticed what was going on in the world. I wanted to have something to say.

At eleven, I started writing poetry about the Vietnam war. Both of my brothers were overseas in a place I could not imagine. I would occasionally contribute a piece of my candy to the box we sent to them every few months. I never asked if they ever received any of it the few times they came home on leave. I just noticed they didn't seem to fit when they came back, like they had become too big to hang out in the kitchen and tell stories.

I began forging an identity outside of my family. I let my processed hair return to its natural state and, in sixth grade, sported my first afro like Angela Davis's. I tried smoking, and I smoked pot after school. My friend's parents had a winning combination of easily accessible pot and a vending machine business. To this day, I cannot eat or even contemplate a Mars Bar.

I was still the "good" student, but I began exploring my edges. I saw the divisions in my high school—jock, nerd, scholar, theater, rah-rah, "bad" influencers. I chose between the theater and being a rah-rah. My endgame in high school was to be on the drill team. When I didn't make it in a vetted tryout, I instead tried out in front of the whole school and became what we called a "song girl." Song girls were a cross between cheerleaders and the drill team. We had sassy little uniforms and pompoms, and we danced to music rather than to the marching band.

In my big theater debut, I played the Black character Tituba in *The Crucible*, Arthur Miller's play about the Salem witch trials. I also got to be the maid (and stole the show) in the musical *George M.* I milked the line sung to my employer, "In a minute, honey," and delighted the audience each night.

My endgame for high school was shortsighted. I just intended to finish. In March of my senior year, the dean of girls scrambled to find me a scholarship and a university after she learned I had no college plans.

Higher education wasn't on my radar because it had never been mentioned to me. My mother's answer to the purpose of my existence was to marry a religious boy, work hard for God, and get to heaven someday. My mother was a Jehovah's Witness and threatened to bar me from going to the university because it was a Jesuit school. Jehovah's Witnesses viewed all other churches as being "of the world" and not the "truth."

I was not interested in that story. At seventeen, I left home, escaping a planned beating. I never went back, heading instead for an adventure where I had no destination in mind.

The day before I left home, my mother had planned a meeting with the admissions people at Santa Clara University. I couldn't reason with her, so I took twenty-seven Excedrin tablets to get her attention. I remember looking at myself in the mirror and feeling numb as I swallowed one pill at a time. Prior to this I couldn't swallow even one pill. And while I was determined to get my message across, I didn't want to die. So I called my sister immediately, and she took me to the hospital. The psychiatrist who examined me said in effect, "You're fine. Your mother is crazy."

When I returned home from the hospital, my mother had arranged for the rest of the family to go out to dinner. I was left alone, retching into a bucket. Later on the phone, she described to a friend how she was going to "beat the shit out of me" for such a stupid stunt. I packed my bag and went out the back door.

Leaving home at seventeen without a plan, I fell into the arms of a young man searching for his own plan. We married when I was eighteen and he was twenty-one. At nineteen, in the midst of my sophomore year in college, I gave birth to my twin children. I finished college, and by the time I finished, I was getting a divorce and jumping into the workforce as a single mom of two. The endgame in my twenties was to survive.

The Goalposts Began to Shift

In my third decade, my end target moved toward accumulation and more accomplishment. Armed with a university degree and honors, I dove into work in the Silicon Valley because they paid well. My brief idea to be a teacher seemed not economically feasible. By the time I graduated, I was twenty-one with two-year-old twins and going through a divorce. Teaching required a year as a student teacher, and the limited pay would not take care of my children.

So I made a left turn and jumped into a world that held no calling for me except the possibility of paying my bills. I stayed and progressed in the Silicon Valley for twenty-five years. I received awards, accolades, stock, bonuses, and more and more pay. I lived in nice neighborhoods, enrolled my kids in good daycare, and accumulated all the material things I thought were the prize.

I married again at twenty-eight. My husband was a romantic Italian who adored my son and daughter and fell in love with me. I worked on the marriage, worked on being a good mom, and took no time to work on me. I left this second marriage, which gave me a dear son and a newfound love of Italy, even as the love for my Italian husband waned.

I thought I had reached the pinnacle. We had everything, but I felt empty inside. I recently watched some videos shot during this period, and it was so obvious I was depressed. A young woman with no vitality in her voice, her step, or her eyes.

Going into my fourth decade, I began to question how much more stuff, money, travel, experiences, and accolades could add to my feelings of happiness or joy. I wasn't feeling joyful; I was feeling driven. I was feeling like I did after binging on cookies or drinking too much tequila or wine. At the moment, I thought I was having fun, then realized I only felt bloated and empty at the same time.

Toward the end of my second marriage, I revealed to myself that my sexuality was oriented toward women. Once divorced, I went off to explore my new identity.

Living as a lesbian in my late thirties didn't keep me from behaving like a teenager. I made up for all the playing I didn't do in college, since I was already a mother. Like a kid in a candy store, I found women of all flavors, sizes, and varieties.

During this period, my endgame was to discover my own desires, interests, and appetites. During one exceptionally randy period, I had three playmates going at once. While they were never in the same room or bed, they were in the same day a few times. I exhausted myself after a few years of this and after a significant relationship with one woman. I looked at my life, trying to figure out what was missing and what was next.

Creating a Love Affair with Life

Moving into my fifth decade gave me the courage to live more out loud and design a life that seemed more congruent with who I was, who I am. I am a singer, songwriter, writer, speaker, minister, facilitator, coach, and leader. I embraced a partner who loved and supported all my aspects. She was full of life and joy and chose me to share it with. She wanted me to be happy and fulfilled, and I vowed to trust her and stay with her through growth and challenges.

I was conscious going into this marriage, unlike my previous ones. I cried outside the church before marrying each of my children's fathers. And I never completely committed to my eight-year relationship to the first woman I loved. At forty-six years of age, I was feeling deep gratitude as I walked toward my wife into our backyard garden on our wedding day.

It seemed most important at this time to live fully. To express, to share, to follow my heart, and to love more openly and sincerely. I found some success in this decade. My relationship thrived and did not end as the others had. In previous relationships, I withheld a good part of myself, not trusting, keeping my bag packed in the event of a necessary exit.

We had some rough spots, she and I. There were a few close calls that if one of us hadn't reached into the chasm dividing us, we might have fallen into despair. But we learned to feel when our hearts were open and when they were closed. We learned to hate the feeling of a closed heart so much that we would do anything necessary to get ourselves available again. Most of the causes were old wounds triggered by a word, an omission, or even a look.

We each did the work on ourselves to heal and lessen the times when something historical made us hysterical in the moment. I remember nights keeping her up, trying to wear her down, my need to be right outweighing my desire for peace. I remember choices she made that felt like a stab in my heart, and in one case, I held that against her for years.

But we made it through because we did the work on ourselves to remove barriers to love inside us. That doesn't mean we have it all figured out, but we strive to love each other more than we each love being right. And we want for each other fulfillment rather than control, so we have a chance for loving-kindness to prevail.

My love affair with Jane and my love affair with our lives continues to provide cues for what matters and what is meaningful.

And still, the question, "To what end?," continues to be alive in me. All the learning in each of my years of life led me to this one. While I can regret some of my choices, I can't change any of them. I look back on my decades and know that I did my best with what I knew to do at the time.

And I'm beginning to realize that maybe figuring it all out is not what I'm here for. Maybe the end target should continue to keep moving so I keep growing.

Does the Target Have to Keep Moving?

chapter 3

As I enjoy the first years of my sixth decade, I wonder if there is some settling, some centering, some feeling of arrival that can happen. Have I hit the target enough or close enough to just sit with life as it is now and not "try" anymore?

I don't feel any sense of arrival or progress or even slowing down on the search for meaning in my life. If anything, the inquiry gets more intense every day. There are times, however, when there is no target, when there is no destination. These are times when I am immersed in the moment. Nature always brings me these moments, so I crave time to rest, breathe, and be among the trees.

At our home in Italy, a river runs through the town. It goes for miles and miles. The clever Italians placed benches and tables and even rubbish bins all along the way. I do as the Italians expect: I wander. I walk. I sit, look, and enjoy.

Feral cats line the path in certain sections. They tiptoe forward to see if you are one of the people who keeps them fed. Fellow walkers pass you, chatting in Italian or another language, some letting their dogs pull them along. Occasionally, I see a family on bikes with a baby facing forward, strapped in a chair. Often I run into the fishermen and women. I have never actually seen anyone catch anything, but I see them sit, hold, watch, and wait every day.

I relish all of these scenes, but what I appreciate the most are the trees.

The trees and bushes that line the river provide shade and give my heart peace. Some are laden with fruit, like the figs that ripen in the sun. Some bushes thrust berries within your reach. Others with ancient trunks stand resolute and silent, witnessing your passing. When I walk, I smile from the inside out. Everyone who passes me sees my smile, and most can't help but greet me with theirs.

What Should I Be Doing Instead?

Isn't this enough, to be alive and walk in nature in gratitude and appreciation? What if that were my assignment every day? Would it meet my criteria of doing no harm and doing some good?

But what about everything going on in human existence while I walk? Shouldn't I take the whole into consideration? How can I have a peaceful walk while somewhere children are starving, abused, or suffering without shelter or any freedoms?

This question haunted me through most of my life. Whatever I was doing, accomplishing, enjoying, or being, whatever it was was never in itself enough. As I write today, I feel tension in my lower back. This tension signals that I am holding something that weighs heavily on me. It could be that our fifth grandchild will be born any moment now, and we are thousands of miles away. It could be that while I am enjoying the view of the river and the Umbrian hills, I should be out getting something done.

My Apple watch says I've had zero minutes of exercise out of a minimum of thirty. I want this pain in my back to go away. I want to feel OK about sitting and writing and making another cup of coffee. But the world calls, and I get up to accomplish something, even if it's just a little yoga.

Our bodies were created to move, so there is that natural impetus. But what if the tension in my back and the call to "go" is a distraction? What part of me wants to sit and write and read and sip a hot beverage right now? Do I listen to that part of me, or do I follow the pain and move?

What Is the Vision?

There is an expression attributed to a spiritual leader, Michael Bernard Beckwith. He said pain pushes until vision pulls. Perhaps vision is the target after all.

What is my vision for my life? And if I am clear about it, does it pull me without pain? And if I am clear about it, is it immutable, or is it still a moving target?

Does your vision for your life square with being one with the whole of Life? Wouldn't my vision and my life have to include the whole?

Emma Curtis Hopkins, a somewhat obscure teacher from the 1920s and 1930s, is someone I have come to appreciate. Among her lessons was one of my favorites: "If you have a clear idea of how a sweet life, free and unburdened, must be, look to this science to bring you this life. Declare very plainly that sweet, free life is mine."

My wife and I adopted the idea of sweet, free life and continually check in to see if we are living it according to the wisdom in each of our hearts. When I define sweet, free life for myself, I mean a life without internal discord. It is no longer about what I am doing or not doing, being or not being, having or not having, but whether I am peaceful within myself. This, to me, is now sweet free Life.

I once had the vision of being able not to work as my end goal. As it turns out, I like to work. And by work, I mean making a contribution of some kind. I coach leaders who do the vital work of helping change oppressive systems to free more people into the possibility of living their own visions. I write songs, produce events, and write and speak inspirational words that, hopefully, expand people's hearts and minds. My current vision is to devote myself to the work of my choosing and that which uses the best of me.

I'd love to say I am beyond accomplishment, but I am not. I'd love to say that it doesn't matter what anyone else thinks of me, because it does. But with passing time, in this human experience, I am moving beyond.

I am moving beyond targets rather than watching targets move beyond my reach. To what end? Perhaps to no end.

No End in Sight

chapter 4

Even though I know there is an unknown expiration date on this body, there is no end in sight for the purpose and meaning in my life. No matter how many years more I live, I will not arrive. How can I be so sure of this? While I can't be sure of anything, I feel something that has become real for me: I see the horizon and know I will never reach it.

It seems human consciousness is not unlike the universe—constantly expanding because that is its nature. My consciousness continually creates because that is its nature. There is no completion in infinity.

This concept is nearly impossible to wrap my head around, but something in me knows it. There is no completion in infinity. Therefore, I believe there is nothing for me to complete.

There must be thousands of books that offer advice on what you need to do to have a fulfilling life. Another thousand books tell you how to do it. What if there is nothing for you to do because life itself is your fulfillment? And the experience is the end? Each moment, each breath—an inhale and an exhale—is its own a tiny universe of life. What if this life is lived from one breath to the next until, finally, the breath does not come?

Trust the Process

I had the privilege of being with a dear friend when she took her last breath. I can recall every detail. Her eyes gently closed, her hands relaxed, the tiny sips of breath she took, and the lengthening seconds between. Then the stillness and the silence. She ended her communication with us through a body. Later, I would feel her communicate as essence, as memory, as energy, as an idea.

When the spirit leaves the body, the body remains illuminated for some time. I wanted to shake her shoulders and say, "Come back! Wake up! I still see you in there." Instead, we bathed her body, anointed it with oils, and looked on, amazed at the peace in her face, the years erased.

Had my friend arrived at the place she was seeking? Or had she continued on her journey without the form we could see? I hear her voice whenever I bring my attention to her in my mind. It is as clear as day and in alignment with the person I know. She says to me, "Keep writing, Christie. Your wisdom is needed. Trust the process."

Trust the process. I can't imagine greater wisdom than this. What if we trust that we are in process at all times?

Where should I put my attention if there were no destination? What if I put my attention on what is good? What if I put my attention on where I am grateful? What if I focus on what I can give to this experience?

I would not run out of good to notice. I would not run out of reasons to be grateful. I would not run out of opportunities to give. A colleague of mine wrote in a magazine recently, "God can use all that I am." He was pointing out that we don't have to be perfect, but we can express the Creator in our own unique ways.

Offering an Alternative Way

We don't have to be perfect to be integral to life on this planet. As spirits enclosed in bodies having a human experience, we will not be ideal. We will be messy and full of noise. Can I say we can avoid being murderers of physical bodies or inflictors of pain while we inhabit emotional bodies? Even this we don't avoid at some level, even if we think of ourselves as good, as loving, as compassionate.

Every day, good people enable and allow the murder of other sentient beings. I do nothing to stop the slaughter of animals, living in horrific conditions, for food. I do nothing to stop my government from dropping bombs and withholding food all around the globe.

I blame the greed of politicians and the wealthy and secretly resent and even feel hatred for a few chosen ones. And yet, I am considered one of the "good" ones. The "bad" ones are the people with guns. Their lives overflow with greed, ruthless capitalism, racism, sexism, xenophobia, or homophobia. And we think it's they who must change or the world will be destroyed.

Meanwhile, we can rally against them and think we're doing our part to make the world better. In our hearts, we know that pointing fingers of blame will not solve things. We know that offering an alternative may. The alternative needs to include every living thing. The alternative places no blame but points to solutions. The alternative means doing our own work. One of the things that stood out in my early life's Bible training was the scripture that advises us remove the log from our own eye before worrying about the splinter in your brother's eye.

The alternative—to focus on being better versions of ourselves, more compassionate, loving, forgiving, and kind—may feel like we are not speaking against what is wrong. These are not mutually exclusive. I can work on myself and clear all the obstacles to my own loving nature and still speak out when others are being harmed. It is the way in which I speak out, not as righteousness but as compassion.

But does changing ourselves, becoming more compassionate, really matter? If there is no end in sight as to what we need to accomplish or do with our lives, why bother to change anything? What if we are here to let things run their course and resolve in their own time?

Bear with me here. I know the part of you that longs for environmental, social, and racial justice is crying right now.

You want to do your part to turn the tide that seems to be threatening our very existence. But here's the thing: You will die, and the world will go on. You will die, and whatever you did to make the world kinder, gentler, better by your presence will continue to have a ripple effect. You will die, and whatever you did to contribute to the world's violence, hatred, and greed will continue to have a ripple effect. So do any of us matter?

When I am lost, I turn to history for clues. I see the places where humankind has done better. I see the areas where lessons were applied, where generosity was extended, where justice prevailed. We are evolving as a species. The question is, are we evolving in the right direction? A direction that will allow homo sapiens to enjoy the planet for some time to come? The past doesn't have to predict the future, but it can inform the possibilities.

What haven't we tried? Maybe we can look back for answers.

How the Past Can Be of Service

chapter 5

Competing narratives exist about the past. Spiritual teachers abound who remind you to stay in the present moment, suggesting the past holds nothing for you. Social justice warriors warn that if we don't study history, we will repeat its mistakes into the future. Which is right?

They are both right. It does serve us to stay in the present moment with the present breath and recognize what Eckhart Tolle calls the "eternal now." In the eternal now, there is peace, there is an expansive possibility, and there is a way forward. Remembering that we can always start anew is powerful. This awareness gives us agency, choice, and authorship in our lives. I am ever grateful to understand and use the power of the now moment.

When I feel anxiety or abject fear, I find breathing into the present moment to be a balm. I will sometimes take deep, connected breaths and say to myself: "You are here, sitting in this chair. Your feet are on solid ground. Your mind is connected to your heart, and you have everything you need right now." This type of affirmation helps me calm my nervous system and tap into a capacity to respond to what is in front of me.

The "power of now" prepared me to speak to thousands of employees and share the hard truths of our failure. And this same power allowed me to get up out of my chair and have a response when I watched the horrific murder of George Floyd.

One of the reasons his death started a firestorm of rage worldwide was because it was familiar. The style of execution was different, but the routine disregard for the life of a Black man touched a nerve. Watching the impassive face of a man with light skin kill a man with dark skin reminded us of our past. It reminded us of the context that made that broad daylight murder possible—today.

Initially, after the shock wore off, educators took advantage of the moment. They began to remind people that the foundations laid for this act were in place for centuries. We had to go back and look at the past to understand how we arrived at the present moment.

Ideas have consequences. The perceived inferiority, the less-than-a-human concept perpetuated about people with dark skin, molded a whole society. This concept of less-than-human (codified in the United States' founding documents that counted a Black man as three-fifths of a man) gave rise to behavior in alignment with that stated belief.

Thereby, the newly formed government of the United States deemed it acceptable to enslave others. The government deemed it acceptable and even appropriate to sell off the progeny of the enslaved. It was acceptable to beat and feed scraps to the enslaved. It was acceptable to rape the women and enslave one's own issue, even to the point of selling them to others, who would likewise mistreat and subjugate them.

The established context of inferiority and of some being subhumans was embedded in the psyche of many people of the time. They accepted this as fact and truth. To question it was to examine the life they were living, the wealth they built on the system of slavery. The use of African people enabled enslavers (and others) to lives full of grandeur; there was a kind of royalty in Southern families. To this day, some embrace the plantation life, the mystique of the southern belle, the song of the South as picturesque, albeit deeply flawed, time in our shared history. They conveniently deny the suffering this life brought to those forced to enable it. They want to remember only the good it brought to their light-skinned families.

The idea of inferiority needs to be kept in place to allow the grand, powerful, wealthy, and prosperous to continue to benefit from it. The concept of inferiority or a type of caste system becomes the social order.

The generational wealth that continues today, built on the backs of enslaved people, has never been reconciled. The families who continue to prosper do not have to account for the lives they stole, the children they sold, the retributions they enacted. We have all seen pictures of the jeering crowds at lynchings after so-called "emancipation."

The laws changed. The minds did not.

The Treatment Must Address the Disease

Many people, Black and White, believe revisiting the pain of this country's foundations is not a helpful exercise. They want to start where we are and provide a remedy.

But here's the thing: You can't offer the treatment without understanding the ravages of the disease. You don't prescribe medicine if you haven't studied the symptoms and the affected systems in the body.

Many times before, our country has attempted to deal with symptoms but not the system. Like with pharmaceuticals, we try to target one symptom and suffer the side effects in our collective body. We applied a salve where deep surgery and recovery were needed. We tried to put bandages on the body and perfume around the stench of entrenched racism. We did not address the idea of inferiority that permeated everything, without which realization change proved impossible.

We must understand that destructive behaviors and consequences result from the mistaken idea of inferiority. Yes, we need laws, incentives, programs, and education, but we need to deal with the root idea before any of this can help us effect change.

Black people, dark-skinned people, have never been in any way inferior. They were never destined for enslavement. They were always whole, sovereign beings who were terrorized and kept down by systemic violence. They were always deserving of freedom and human dignity.

We have to look at the fundamental error in thought that made Black people separate from the rest. By no means are Blacks in America the only example of this fundamental error, but they are a relevant example of why the past must be reviewed before we can heal the present.

Some believe that talking about the victimization of Blacks and looking for a present-day remedy makes Black people weaker. They think it doesn't imbue Blacks with the agency to solve their own problems. I think the problems created by racial hatred and division are not Blacks' own problems. Racial hatred and division were perpetrated and kept in place by those who benefitted from them. Those who profited from the enslavement of Black people or the genocide of Native Americans must be willing to stop benefiting from it for the systems to come crashing down.

These ideas have been explored by eloquent authors and teachers across the globe. I exhort you to read Isabel Wilkerson's book *Caste* and other writings to give you all the context you need to understand where we are.

I mention this example to illustrate the value of looking back when we want to heal a fundamental idea driving our behavior. While we don't want to spend our lives blaming, we do want to understand what may drive others' behaviors, too.

Past as Prelude

The present divide among people was preceded by lies told about the "other," lies about the inherent inferiority of Blacks,

Jews, Indigenous people, women, immigrants, Muslims, and so many others. What is a lie still operating in your life? Your own inferiority? Your own inadequacy? Your own worthlessness? What is keeping you from living your best life now?

When we ask ourselves these questions, we often need to look back in our lives to see when we drew the conclusion from which we now act. Where is the root idea? How are we keeping it in place? When we expose these crumbling ideas to light, we can begin to remove them from their foundation. This is how negative examples can be healed and new life forged.

New life also can be forged by seeing what has worked, what has progressed, and amplifying that. Using the example of race, we can look at the courageous people who defied the system and created an underground railroad to freedom. We can see those who refused to be slave holders. We can look at those who raised their voices and used their power to end it.

Today, we have people making a difference on behalf of the whole in many areas of life. I point to the improvement of rights for Black people and for women as indicators that we can change our ideas and behaviors. We see that there continues to be resistance to the freedom of all people. The purpose of this resistance is constant—to keep the power, privilege, and prosperity where it is, and not allow those who have it to lose anything. This idea is based on faulty logic, the idea that there is not enough for everyone. We can look around the world and find many examples where believing there is enough for everyone can be the creative juice for finding the solutions.

The lessons of the past can be used to inform the present. Choose your lessons wisely, but do take the opportunity to learn. What ideas drive your behavior today? What beliefs about yourself were handed down to you? Notice where your heart feels closed and you don't feel peace. Breathe into those feelings and discover their source. Again, this is not to blame someone in the past but to free yourself from living wounded in the present.

What About My Personal Past?

chapter 6

If history can be used to direct social action today, our personal experiences can be used to inform our pursuit of peace. One of the ways I look to my past for lessons is in noticing what I was after, what I hoped to accomplish, whether I got or achieved it, and whether getting it was all I expected.

At seventeen, I wanted to leave home to escape what I considered an oppressive environment. I left home and married at eighteen, only to find in a few years that I needed to free myself from that environment as well.

After graduating college, all I wanted was a good paying job. The good paying job turned into twenty-five years of my life working in technology instead of learning anything about who I was and what I came here to do. I left corporate life only to discover that my addiction to achievement moved with me.

During my corporate years, I had exposure to different ideas of spirituality and religion. After my experiences growing up, I lost trust and interest in the organized religion I had been exposed to. I wanted to have a deeper spiritual understanding, so I studied to be a minister, but found (after five years of intensive training) that being in a church every Sunday was not my calling.

As I write this, I sit on a park bench overlooking a river in central Italy. The birds are prolific, the fishermen and women quiet, and I am appreciating how I came to be here enjoying a healthy, prosperous adventure.

I created my current life out of the ones that did not work for me. For decades I achieved but did not believe in my worthiness to enjoy. During my twenties and thirties, I woke up most mornings feeling a weight on my heart that I did not know how to ease. All I could do, all I knew how to do was to stay in motion and hope I wouldn't succumb to the dark that threatened to close over my life. I received some help through therapy and other types of spiritual growth work, strategies that saved my life long enough for me to find a way to live with myself.

Let's Discard Our Self-Hatred

I spent a lot of time suffering, but my exterior presence suggested there was no reason for it. Sadly, this is not uncommon. People who have terrible circumstances, whether poverty or living in warlike conditions, can be happier than someone who is relatively wealthy and safe. Why? Because our lives are in our own minds.

I chose suffering due to ideas I picked up in my past, ideas I did not take time to examine and then discard. We need to examine what we believe and have the courage to discard what we know to be either untrue or violent.

It is untrue that any mistakes you or I have made are irredeemable. It's untrue that you or I are not worthy of love or success.

It is violent to believe that you or I deserve to suffer. It is violent not to care for your own body or well being. While wars rage on across the planet, too many of us walk around at war with ourselves. These inner conflicts inform and add to the outer. These inner conflicts reduce our capacity to help with anything happening in the world.

Discard the Past to Become a Beacon

If you have a clear idea of how sweet life, free and unburdened, must be, look to this Science to bring you this life. And declare very plainly that sweet, free life is your Good.

~ Emma Curtis Hopkins,
Scientific Christian Mental Practice

As I look at my past and take inventory, I find much to discard. I discard any self-hatred learned from people who were afraid of or ashamed of my Blackness, including my mother. I discard my lack of self-worth perpetuated by men who took my body for their own pleasure without acknowledging my inherent dignity. I discard the words of people who told me I was too much of this and too little of that.

I discard the shame of not being Black enough and sounding like I wanted to be White. I discard the need to suffer in order to show that I care about my ancestors.

I discard the need to apologize for living a "sweet and free life." I discard the need to accomplish in order to be valuable. I discard the need to rehearse in case the proverbial other shoe drops. I discard the need to be great at something in order to do it. I discard the judgement. I discard my struggle about what is enough generosity.

I discard needing to make up for what my mother did not experience in her mostly miserable life.

It really doesn't matter where the ideas came from. What matters is whether these ideas enable us to live lives in which we restore peace on the inside.

This is my main focus—achieving peace on the inside. Any past experience or idea that operates in opposition to my peace, I must discard.

What part of your past holds onto you? What does it feel like to put it down, release it, discard it? Maybe transformation is a more powerful idea for you. If so, how can you transform ideas from ones that don't serve your inner peace to ones that do?

One thing that helps me create more inner peace and calm is to recognize that my suffering on behalf of others does nothing to relieve their suffering. More people than I can count say things like this to me: "Thank you for sharing your beautiful life. You give me something to aspire to." "You give me hope that joy is around the corner." "I appreciate that you understand all the hard, bad things happening in the world, and that you can still find reasons to be grateful."

If I can lift another person for one moment, this is good. If I can keep one person from a sea of despair long enough for them not to drown, this is good. If I can be a beacon of another way of being, I am deeply grateful.

You can be a beacon to help folks find more inner peace by finding your own. We can be compassionate without having to share the experience other folks have. We can be kind and loving without checking our own joy at the door.

What a powerful way to use our past. Transform what did not work into new ideas and amplify what did work to spread more good in the world.

Reach back and celebrate those things that bring you joy, gratitude, and feelings of love. Reach back and release those things that bring you guilt, remorse, fear, or sadness. You are worthy of a peace-filled existence, in spite of all that may have occurred and in spite of what else is going on in the world. The whole needs your peace.

How Important Is the Plan?

chapter 7

I have fallen in love with so many plans for my life. When I was young my plan was to be a wildly successful writer, have no children, and travel the world. I had twin children at nineteen, have only just now begun working as a writer, and I've done a fair amount of traveling the world. A plan gave shape to my days and helped me put one foot in front of the other, even if I felt lost or unsure. A plan was tidy and connected to my mind, but it was not always in touch with my heart.

What difference does it make if you create a plan and either complete it or miss the mark? I wonder. Life has a way of unfolding in front of you, and you either can notice the cues and follow them or forge ahead and follow your plan.

Early in my life, I feared failure. I had two little ones depending on me, so I quickly let go of following my intuition and dreams and desires. Even though I followed my plan to earn an income sufficient to care for my two children in my early twenties, my dreams kept rearing their heads.

When I was in my late twenties, I started writing. I wrote a hundred pages about my life to that point. I wrote about the good, the bad, and the ugly. I told my second husband how I dreamt of writing, and he said, "You are not a kid anymore. You need to give up that dream and realize you are a mother (now of three) and that should take your focus and attention."

Our marriage didn't make it after eight years for lots of reasons, but one of them was that I began to assert myself and step out, following my callings. One calling led me to become a local elected leader. I remember him saying then, "We cannot have two lions in the house." My sovereignty and power were on the prowl, and he thought he could cage me. But it didn't work. I broke out, and we broke up. None of this was part of the plan.

If I had followed my instincts, I wouldn't have married either of the men I did. Both times, someone found me crying outside the church. These were not sweet tears. My body was screaming, "*Stop!*," and in trying to ignore it, the emotion flooded out of my eyes. Every true fiber of my being knew I was not in alignment with myself to marry these men.

At the time I did not know—and was perhaps unwilling to know—why. I followed the plan, and I received the great gift of my three children. But I only followed those plans for a time. My first marriage ended after three years and the second after eight.

My current marriage to a woman did not include any tears before going to the altar. We have been together nearly twenty years. I never planned to be with a woman, let alone marry one, but this has been one of the greatest adventures of my life.

Discernment Removes Regrets

I do not harbor any regrets about following my former plans. I can't. I received so much good from those marriages. I love my children with all my heart, and I know I am a better human being because of them.

It seems there are gifts, whether you follow the plan or follow your heart. I think following your heart can also bring you the gifts you desire, and you may not need to experience the suffering that can come from forcing yourself to follow a plan.

This is where discernment comes in. We have to discern when our plan is in alignment with our hearts. Do we feel a sense of peace or do we feel inner conflict when we contemplate the path in front of us? Take a deep breath and look at your life. Are you in the midst of following a plan? How does it feel? Are you just taking one day at a time? How does that feel?

Right now, I experience the fruits of a plan to stay in Italy for the full ninety days allowed. I am so happy here that it seems in rock solid alignment with my heart. And yet my new granddaughter was born the other day, and I'm thousands of miles away. If I could beam myself there and back, I would do it. Does this pull away from my life in Italy mean I am off my aligned path? I think not. I think this is life. We constantly make choices and course corrections in deciding what will we do, be, or have. And we are capable of feeling more than one emotion at a time. I can miss you and still be happy where I am.

Let Your Heart Speak

I think the magic is in the mystery. Have a plan, but hold it lightly. See what signs show up, what nudges you feel. Play on the road of your life. If we keep our heads down, we miss the beauty along the way. Look up and around. Notice. Take a pause. And then step into the next moment.

Sometimes you have a plan that seems aligned with your heart's desires—until it doesn't. What to do then? Close your eyes. See yourself following the path you currently are on. What do you see and how do you feel? Imagine yourself taking a turn off this path toward something else. What is the something else? How does it feel? And then, if you can, sit with the uncertainty for a little while. Don't decide immediately. Let your heart speak and give you the words that help you decide the next step.

If you know someone who seems to be lost and is not making progress in your view or that of the world, look again. Maybe they are learning the signs, trying to find the way that makes their heart sing. None of us does this journey of life the same way. We all have our own unique experience. And that experience primarily happens in our own minds.

Focus on staying in alignment with your own heart, and check in regularly. Bless all your fellow journeyers. Wish them a good path, and this wish will return to you.

To Love Deep
or to Love Wide?

chapter 8

I realize in asking the question in the chapter title in this way means I believe the choice is binary. One or the other. I imagine it is possible to love both deep and wide when you train yourself to live, move, and have your being immersed in Love, immersed in the energy that fuels all life, whether you call it God, Spirit, Nature, or Love. I think this immersion is a level of mastery that we may get glimpses of, but we may not be able to maintain such mastery moment to moment. Using our human limitation as the parameter, let's look at loving deep.

When I say to love deep, I imagine being able to approach unconditional love. I say "approach," again presuming it is a challenge in the human experience to release all judgment and any withholding and still be completely vulnerable.

We express unconditional love when we have no expectation of the other. We love in response to everything we see, hear, or experience. Love is our answer to every question. Love is our reflex. We place no conditions on allowing love to flow through us. This is the ultimate challenge.

I experience unconditional love flowing through me when I am with infants. I don't expect infants to be or do anything other that what they are being and doing. I love them whether they are crying, smiling, laughing, or fussing. I accept them exactly as they are in any moment.

However, I have not sustained this unconditional love once a child is old enough to follow directions and chooses not to. This doesn't mean that correcting a child or trying to modify their behavior for their safety is not loving. It means I begin to respond with fear, concern, and a need to control, rather than with a sense of love. I begin to want them to be different than what they are being. I want them to be more agreeable and not to throw tantrums. I want them to quickly learn not to bite or throw. And I become impatient.

In my imagination, a child who is unconditionally loved experiences correction as a tender admonition. They are shown the best way to do things, and they respond to loving correction with love. This is my imagination because I was not a perfectly unconditionally loving parent.

I also sometimes experience unconditional love for nature. In whatever form it comes, I find myself feeling appreciation for nature and the cosmos. Whether a storm or a balmy, sunny day, I love what nature brings. When I place my hand on the trunk of a tree, I feel a unity and a connection that takes my breath away. This gives me an idea of what deep, abiding love feels like.

Where I find myself adding conditions is to the life of insects. I can love all of nature, as long as mosquitos don't buzz and bite and creepy crawly things don't come into my home. I have not mastered unconditional love for all living things to be sure.

And then there are humans. What if living is about loving at least one human being deeply? We are so flawed. We have neuroses, irritating habits, imperfect communication, and sometimes unreasonable, exasperating requirements. This describes the best of us. The *worst* of us have all of the above, and destructive habits, meanness, unmanaged emotions, selfishness, greed, and other vices.

And so loving a human being deeply, without withholding for any condition, could be a pinnacle of one's life.

What Responding with Love Looks Like

What could loving deep look like? Responding to whatever is presented with love. For example, your mate or friend needs to control all the conditions in their life, including you. They constantly give instructions, corrections, and suggestions. You respond with love. "Thank you for these instructions, corrections and suggestions." Your mate or your friend is unhappy. You respond with love. "I see you are suffering. How can I help you?" Your mate or your friend is not loving toward themself. You respond with love. "My beloved, you are so easy to love."

How do we know we are responding with love? I have learned to recognize when my heart is open and when it is closed or protected. Opening your heart leaves you vulnerable. You can literally feel this vulnerability. Open your arms wide, and breathe into the area around your heart. Notice if you want to close your arms over your chest. Notice if it feels uncomfortable to be wide open.

When I open my arms wide, I feel a surge of energy. I sense emotions rising to the surface of my awareness. Sometimes the emotions feel like what we perceive as good emotions. I feel gratitude, joy, contentment, happiness. Other times, a feeling of heaviness arises. It seems to block me like a protective wall being erected.

If I continue to breathe through the heaviness, I can allow tears to flow or anger to subside or even rage to run its course. I need not be afraid of feeling all I have stored inside me. What is stored can wreak havoc if it's not released.

I don't need to judge what I feel; I need only allow it. If I resist the feelings of anger, rage, or deep despair that arise, I enable them to become more powerful in me. My resistance fuels anger, resentment, and literally inflames my body. When I finally let myself feel, after resisting, sometimes the feelings come out in a chaotic, haphazard, sometimes harmful way. They can harm me or someone who happens to be in my presence because they were left so long to fester.

I have gotten much better about managing my emotions and allowing them air so they can be transformed. This way, I am not taken for a ride by my emotions. I let them dissipate.

Open your arms again right now. Breathe into that area of your heart. Breathe through any discomfort. You will thrive on the other end of this experience. When you take time to clear your heart of stored emotion regularly, then your heart can remain open and receptive to allowing love to flow through it.

The Vibration of Love

Love is an allowing. You can choose in any moment to allow it into your being. It is always present as a force, as an energy. You don't have to generate or create it. You just need to be aware of it.

Close your eyes, if you need to. Recall a time when you felt love. Breathe into that.

This opening can allow you to love more deeply. You can love more deeply because you've opened yourself to a reservoir of an endless substance. As you allow more to flow through you, the same flows to others in your life.

One of the most powerful examples of unconditional love I have witnessed is with friends who have an animal family. One of my friends has had Bernese mountain dogs for the past thirty years. They are so large and have a limited life span, inherent in the breed. Often they die within eight to ten years. Each dog is loved so deeply by my friend. I see them curled up together on the floor. I see the joy each experiences when they encounter the other. And I see the deep concern when my friend or the dog experience a health challenge. The dog stays faithfully by my friend's side, and he faithfully attends to his dog's needs, no matter the time or place. When death is imminent—which it always is after seven, eight, or nine years—I watch my friend grieve. I see his heartbreak, and then I see his willingness to do it all again. I have known him through five losses, and I am in awe of his heart that opens and opens and opens again and again, knowing what he'll need to suffer through to have the experience.

While the length of time we will have human family and friends is unknown, we can love them more fully with an open heart.

With a fullness of love in your heart, you give attention to the beloved in your life, whether that is a romantic partner, a family member, or a friend. This approach to engage with the other with an open heart can make for a much different relationship.

The beloved other becomes a way for you to experience love. Everything you give is returned to you. You must have courage to love someone deeply. Doing so means to love without condition. It means to love all of what you see and experience. It means to allow that person to fully express, right where they are as they are, instead of wanting them to be different. It means to risk loss.

Science tells us that the vibration of love energy is creative and powerful. As you allow it in you, you experience it as you and as your life. With your heart open, look into the eyes of one, giving everything you have. Is this deep giving the end for which we live?

And Then, Go Wide

What about loving wide? What if we can allow love to flow through and across to every person we are aware of and we are not aware of? If we unconditionally apply open heartedness to everything we encounter, is this the endgame that makes us winners in life? What would be possible if we each were to have an open heart toward every living thing on the planet?

Often I thought I could not manage this much energy moving through me. I imagined that if you operate at the level of constant unconditional love, you vibrate off the planet because it's too much for your body to hold. This is what keeps me from faithfully and fully practicing the presence of love every day. I actually fear its power.

Yet, this could be the end that our human life directs us toward—noticing that there are no answers except love. Loving wide means love is our response to everything that happens. Some days, I can imagine this; and some days, it feels ridiculous. More of us being ridiculous could be a very good thing.

The Process
of Elimination

In contemplating what I am here for, I now can see the things I am not here for. For example, I am not here to accumulate things. The bumper sticker I saw on a fancy car that reads, "He who dies with the most toys wins," is a lie. He who dies with the most toys likely missed out on the real prize of life: the experience of love for the sake of love.

This is not to say that a wealthy person cannot experience the boundlessness of love. But it is to say that the pursuit of wealth can sometimes get in the way. What does that scripture say? In Matthew 19:24, Jesus says, "it is easier for a camel to go through the eye of a needle than for a rich person to enter the kingdom of God."

Not being here to accumulate things doesn't mean I am not prosperous. The universe is unlimited in its ability to generate wealth of all kinds. I can play in that unlimited field and still remain open to love. With a wide open heart I'm also likely to look for ways to generate good with my good. I imagine that if I leave the planet with less than I have now, it would be because I distributed more of it, not because my abundance lessened in any way.

The question, "To what end?", is not answered by any thing. That's easy to say and understand. It's more challenging to say it's also not answered by any accomplishment, especially when the accomplishment helps others or makes things more beautiful.

Is my art, writing, or service the end for which I am here? If someone doesn't make art, write, or serve others in any discernible way, was their life less than worthy?

I know people, including myself, who received awards and accolades, all while struggling with self-hatred or abject terror or fear for their lives. Were those accomplishments real?

I know people, including myself, who reach pinnacles in their careers, who hit the salary or bonus target time and again but still feel empty inside. I imagine some of the wealthiest people on Earth continue to search for their version of contentment or inner peace.

I have met a few people, my wife included, who feel a deep sense of contentment and thus feel ready to exit this life at any time. They found an inner peace, a level of satisfaction, a knowing that their physical existence is only a fraction of who they are.

My wife knows she doesn't need one more possession. She knows she doesn't need to accomplish one more thing. She flows from yoga pose to yoga pose and feels herself wholly and completely immersed in love as life.

Without accomplishing anything other than completing her practice for the day, she knows she does no harm. She knows she contributes peace into the collective by cultivating her own peace. She knows.

Not things, not accolades, not attaining a specific level of accomplishments or finding just the right set of circumstances satisfies the question, "To what end?" I have what 99% of the world's people might consider everything. I have two beautiful homes, and all the accompanying accoutrements. I have a loving spouse, loving children, and loving grandchildren. I have the freedom to travel. I have excellent health and access to whatever I need to maintain it. I have skills and people who want to work with me. And working is optional for me.

I have an extraordinary life. And yet I pursue what those who don't have shelter or prospects pursue once their primary needs are settled—peace and the experience of love.

I have friends who intentionally live without a home. They are nomads, traveling to wherever their hearts call them from day to day. I can think of one who experiences more peace on any given day than I do with all my perfect external circumstances. She greets each new day with a renewed commitment to accept with grace each thing that shows up and transform it into growth toward greater love. What an intention! To be used and to use everything toward greater and greater expressions of love. What a purpose!

Is the Purpose the Thing?

Is the purpose the thing itself? Is asking for purpose and asking, "To what end?", saying the same thing? I would say it is not. Purpose implies there is a template for each person and they need only discover it and follow it. What if we create a new template with our own hearts and minds by what we focus on every day? If I were to agree that purpose is the end we seek, the only purpose could be love. It is unlimited and absolute.

You could say, "I know folks who were born to be this or that." I just watched a program about a sixteen-year-old doctor who graduated from medical school when she was fourteen. You could say it was her purpose to be a doctor. It was her purpose to pursue healing others, which begs the question: If she, for any reason, became incapable of this practice, who would she be and to what end would she be living?

No, we can't take a fixed purpose and say that as long as we realize and execute that, we must be answering our life's call. I return again to the idea that to love deep and/or wide is life's call. Answering that call doesn't require any skill, money, status, position, circumstance, location, gender, or bodily configuration. It requires only a willingness to be used by love.

To be used by love helps us eliminate anything that tries to use us to hate or to separate. In this way, we can use the process of elimination to discover to what end we are here. If it separates, judges, harms, excludes, or entertains fear, it is *not* what we are here to do.

Listen. What calls do you hear from your heart? Is your heart wide open? What would it take to allow it to open? What if a wide-open heart is the only goal?

Living with an Open Heart

chapter 10

When I think of living with an open heart, I first think of a child. I remember the Stevie Wonder song, "With a Child's Heart." He sings:

With a child's heart
Nothing can ever get you down
With a child's heart
You've got no reason to frown
Love is as welcome
As a sunny, sunny day
No grown-up thoughts
To lead our hearts astray

Just imagine. "Love is as welcome as a sunny day, and no grown-up thoughts to lead our hearts astray."

Grown-up thoughts—like being responsible, protecting ourselves from being hurt, waiting for the other to make the first move so we don't look foolish—these thoughts get in the way of welcoming the love that presses itself all around us. Living with an open heart is like living with an open door. We learned to close, lock, fortify, alarm, and create double barriers to our homes. Unfortunately, we also learned to do this within.

I am of the generation that is always lamenting about the "good old days," when we were allowed as children to go out in the morning and come back at dinnertime. The door was open, and we were free to explore.

I came to know my true self because I could get on my bike and go search for the end of the rainbow, following it for miles. I appreciated trees and nature and the bounty of the earth by climbing fences and snatching warm peaches in the sun. I explored the edges of risk by walking inside a cement tunnel with the freeway roaring above my head. When I came home, I simply walked in, just as my friends walked into their homes.

I can remember knocking on neighbors' doors to see if someone could come out and play. There was no sound of locks clicking, and I didn't have to knock on a wrought-iron screen door. The neighbors just opened their doors. And in the summertime, just a simple screen door was between my face and theirs. I lived in suburbs, and I realize that in urban environments, doors were locked more often. But there was a time when we trusted each other more and felt safer.

Leaving the door open didn't mean you would get robbed or raped or have some other tragic thing happen. Leaving the door open said, "Welcome." It could mean you'd find a pie waiting on your table or even an unexpected guest in your chair. The door could be open just to welcome you to your own home without juggling keys and locks.

Unlock Your Heart

Depending on our history, our experiences, and our resulting mindsets, our hearts can feel like a safe country or a scary city. We keep our heart double bolted, barred with an iron screen, when we have seen, heard, or experienced violence around us or directed at us. We keep our hearts locked behind a heavy wall if we have been hurt in a relationship, whether physically or emotionally. Sometimes our hearts are closed because of our ancestral memory within our very cells.

We become so accustomed to the door being closed that we don't honestly remember what if feels like to have it open —what it feels like to let the breeze of fresh new experiences come in, what it feels like to be embraced or invited in for a warm meal or conversation. We keep our hearts closed because that's what feels familiar, and the familiar can feel safe.

It feels risky to open the doors of our hearts. But, oh, what riches await us. Sending out the vibration of love with an open heart is like a melody that draws good to you. I fondly remember the ice cream truck in my childhood. We would hear the distant tinkling of the old song that played over and over as it came closer and closer. The truck would arrive around our corner to find a gaggle of kids jostling for the first position in line. We knew something good was coming. We *expected* something good.

Good will gather and come running toward you when you open your heart. An open heart magnetizes what matches its vibration. The vibration of an open heart is full of light and forward-moving energy. An open heart invites unlimited gifts. Around every corner and in each breath there is an opportunity for more good to show up.

The more we use our open hearts, the more they expand our capacity. For example, I love to sing, but I need to do it daily for my vocal cords have the flexibility and lubrication to deliver the sound. In the same way, our hearts need the exercise of being open to accept all the good that comes our way.

I love the expression, "filled up and flowing over." Our hearts can flow over when we let good keep coming in, when we give from a fullness that seems endless.

Live with Your Heart Open

I often wonder if I can live daily with an open heart. A part of me feels like it would be exhausting, while another part imagines it would be exhilarating.

The thing that tires me out is not open heartedness, it's the fear of being vulnerable when my heart is wide open. This fear is not logical. It comes from the uncertainty of being open to whatever shows up. Even if so much good shows up in my life every day, I continue to brace myself for the "bad" or for the "challenge." This idea is worth getting to the bottom of and releasing.

Good doesn't have to be followed by something bad to counterbalance it. Good can flow continuously and without interruption. In fact, good does exactly that, but we have to monitor to where we put our attention. There is always good flowing. Even if we are in chaos externally, there may be a blue sky or a flower that brings our attention to beauty. Even if we have physical challenges, music may remind us of the gift of our senses.

There is always good. How much can you accept?

I've heard the expressions—"I just can't take it." "It's just too much." "This is too good to be true."—all related to good things happening that open our hearts wider and let in a flood of gratitude. We say we just can't take it and it's too much because we don't know how to accept all the good coming our way. And expanding our capacity for good may feel uncomfortable.

I remember one afternoon at a celebration of a weekend-long event I produced. I sat with a spiritual teacher of mine, and, suddenly, I felt as if my heart would erupt out of my chest. I sensed I was starting to leave my body, or maybe I was going to pass out, or maybe I was having a heart "event." I breathed in deeply and got the message that my heart was, in that moment, undergoing an expansion to accept all the good, the love, the joy that just occurred over the weekend.

I told my teacher I could feel my heart and I knew what was happening. I asked her just to sit with me. Full of wisdom and trust of spirit, she sat quietly as the transformation of my heart into a wider acceptance happened.

I smiled through tears, and she did, too.

Accepting the Fierceness of Love

chapter 11

I read the poetry of the Sufi Hafiz. His words fill me with a sense of timeless gratitude and often make me smile. One of his poems says that sometimes God wants to shake us upside down and let all the nonsense fall out. This made me think of the concept of fierce love. Love that is not kind, gentle, or bearing all things, but instead love that clears anything unlike itself out of the way.

As a mother, I resonate with the idea of love's fierceness. When you believe your child is in any kind of danger, love takes over, and you become a warrior. I've heard stories of mothers and others lifting entire cars to save their beloveds. This energy of love concentrated in action can be overwhelming and even scary.

How can love be fierce? And is it always a force for good?

I sometimes feel afraid, knowing the fierce energy love can become. I temper myself when I get too passionate about something. I stop myself when my reflex is to risk my own life for someone in need. The concepts of "too passionate" and "life at risk" are fabricated in my mind. I have not been in a situation where there is a gun pointing at me or a bomb about to go off. I have never been a first responder who heads willingly into a fire to save others from it. Those are choices made by brave and willing hearts. I imagine that I fear the fierceness of love because it may compel me to do something that seems heroic.

It's only natural to want to preserve our lives. This instinct has been instilled in us. We hear so much about the fight or flight mechanism and how we overuse it. The purpose of the fight or flight mechanism is to keep us alive. It was designed to prompt us to run or defend our lives when a threat is present. As we have all heard and read over and over, many people in our modern society perceive daily life itself as a threat. With warring factions, unhealthy air, economic pressure, and, yes, even a pandemic, we have lots of reasons to feel we need protection.

What we don't need protection from is the impetus of love itself. We don't need to make sure we stay safe from what love may call us to do. She loves fiercely, he loves fiercely, they love fiercely. Fierce without relenting, with all power, with all intention, with our full heart. We imagine something this powerful can consume us. What would be the outcome of being consumed by love? We see bad examples in cinematic glory. The woman or man consumed by love, murders, or destroys their own life in pursuit of the beloved. But this is not love that has consumed them. This is possession.

Love Is the Energy of Life

We do not need to possess the thing we are made from. We are made from the energy of life. This is the definition

I have for love: the energy of life. Like electricity, it is powerful and can be used in any way we chose.

We are the conduits for this love energy that moves all things. To let it have its way with us can be scary, and this is where all the juice of life lies. I become more willing every day to be one with fierce love.

I wrote this chant for an inspiration event I produced a few years ago:

> *Fierce love*
> *Tap into your soul*
> *Fierce love*
> *Tap in to your soul*
> *Fierce love*
> *Tap into power*
> *Strength and glory*
> *Its in your control*
> *Fierce love*
> *Fierce love's not a thing in the sky*
> *Fierce love it's in you and I*
> *Fierce love*

It changes everything....

If we think of love as the force of life and the transforming agent that changes things, we can begin to accept more love flowing into and through our hearts, mainly because we can resist or we can allow. And resisting love or the energy of life doesn't give us anything except tension and stress.

Let's Be Fierce Together

What would it feel like to see the fierceness, the unrelent-ingness of love and to then accept its power as our own lives?

When have you felt fierce? When have you felt the fierceness of love? If this idea is unfamiliar or doesn't make sense or you can't relate to it, what might you be missing?

I remain curious and fascinated about love and its power. I remain curious and fascinated about the idea that love as the power of life is the only true thing. I seek to know love in my heart and as my heart. I want to trust that whatever the life force brings to me, I can transform into growth and into good for myself and others.

This trust can create the opposite of a life that feels man-ageable, under our control, somewhat predictable. We have to decide, as Einstein once queried, whether we believe this to be a friendly or hostile universe—a universe, as opposed to a society or even a world. In the greater context, is the energy of life friendly or hostile?

Fierceness doesn't need to be hostile. Fierceness can be cleans-ing, freeing, and, yes, destructive. In Hinduism, there are Ganesha and Shiva, both transformers and destroyers. They transform and destroy whatever is in the way of pure devo-tion. Shiva destroys, and Ganesha removes obstacles.

Devotion is a state of mind that recognizes the Source of Life and lives in a way that honors the gift of life. This honor includes destroying and removing anything in the way of open-hearted love. To live and give and be a light honors the Source.

Wilding
Your Own Heart

chapter 12

After writing the chant about fierce love, the next year I wrote:

> *Wild hearts*
>
> *Heal the world*
>
> *Wild hearts*
>
> *Set love free*
>
> *Open*
>
> *Feel*
>
> *Fierce love reveal*
>
> *Wild your heart*
>
> *Let love heal*
>
> *Wild hearts...*

Most of us find that our hearts are somewhat familiar territory, at least mine has been. I know where all the secrets are hidden. I know where my sorrows have been buried, I know where my desires live.

I do my best to avoid whatever might open a door to a sorrow, secret, or wound. Some forms of yoga use the term *samscara* to refer to stored emotions, usually those that are painful. This stored energy lives in the heart and takes up space, resulting in our hearts feeling clogged rather than open.

What We Carry in Our DNA

Science supports the idea that our cells actually store memories, not just what happened but how we felt about it and the meaning we assigned to it. So many of us endured abuses or traumas and made ourselves wrong or another person wrong. We still suffer from unexpressed anger, sadness, or rage. Our heart's more natural state, which is open and receptive, can become closed and resistant.

We also hold sorrows and pain from our ancestors. When I visited Selma, Alabama, and walked across the Edmund Pettus Bridge, I felt the fear of those who came before me, some of whom are still alive. When I walked the path of the enslaved ones from the ship to the auction block, I felt their shame and rage. I had so much pain in my emotional body that my physical body could hardly move. And these things—the horrors of enslavement and continual violence—did not actually happen to me in my lifetime. So I carry what happened to my ancestors in my DNA.

Instead of feeling safe and free to let my heart be an open and a safe place through which to explore and experience life, it became a closed gate, intended to limit my exposure to pain. This fortress may feel safe, but it keeps me imprisoned and thwarts my freedom to fully feel all that comes into my life. There are, though, moments where an experience breaks through my barrier.

An Apology to Me, by Me

I remember the first time I was in a plantation home in the state of Georgia. I was the president of a nonprofit board, and one of our members proudly offered the home for a benefit event. I needed to give the opening remarks, but before I was to go on, I had to run out of the house and around a corner to weep.

When I walked into the space, there was a winding staircase. The wood stairs and the floor below literally gleamed. I saw a woman walking down those stairs. She was dressed in a taupe cotton shift with an apron and a cloth tied over her hair. She carried a bucket and rags. I looked into her eyes and she into mine. The depth of her soul poured out from those eyes, and I was compelled to touch the floor in honor of her suffering. Instead, I ran out of the house.

While weeping on the corner of a willow-tree lined avenue of a Savannah suburb, I wrote out an apology to myself from the United States of America.

> *Dear African American, This is the United States of America speaking. We apologize for stealing you from your homeland, tearing your families apart, stacking you as though you were less than animals in the bottom of boats for months, and forcing you to live in the excrement of those around and above you. We apologize for rewarding your survival with being sold into slavery and for the beatings and submission you endured for the purposes of building wealth that you could not access in any way.*

We apologize for requiring you to raise our children while we sold yours as soon as they were old enough to work, or put them to work as soon as they were able to stand. We apologize for hanging your men by their necks on trees for having the audacity to behave like men. We apologize for the rape of your women at the hands of their owners. We apologize for the lie of the church that promised salvation, and we apologize for freeing you but never giving you the freedom to flourish.

We further apologize for now blaming you for your lack of wealth, for your sense of victimization, and for your fear of the ruthless system that made your human life a commodity. We are sorry that we don't know how to undo what we have done.

— Christie, 1998

After I scribbled this statement on paper, I breathed until I knew I could walk back into the space. I must have looked different when I came back because Kevin, the executive director, asked me if I was OK. I said I was not, but I would go on. I told him briefly what happened, and another board member was standing nearby. The other board member swept me up and led me into the kitchen, where caterers were preparing for the afterparty. (They happened to be all White folks.)

He loudly exclaimed, "This is Christie. She is our board president, and right now she needs to boss some White people around." The looks on their faces froze in a mixture of shock and surprise and then relief when I started to laugh. He broke the trance of sadness I was in, and I went out to the crowd and delivered a passionate talk about supporting our lesbian, gay, transgender, and bisexual brothers and sisters in their rights to freedom.

This situation somewhat prepared me for one that happened just a couple of years later, at the turn of the century. I was sitting at a table I was hosting as an award-winning leader in my company. The woman next to me was from an office in the South. I don't remember which city or state, but I remember her accent and words when she turned to me with a sweet smile and said, "I have never sat next to a Black person before." The silence around the table was deafening. And I don't think anyone breathed. I looked at her and asked, "Well, how is it?" She smiled and laughed, and we went on with our dinner.

I wonder how everyone at that table felt about their response or lack thereof. I wonder how she truly felt about my answer. I was in a surreal state the rest of the evening, so I have no idea what else was said at that table. To this day, it rocks me that someone in the year 2000 had the experience of never having a Black person in their presence. And that they were innocent about asking and were open to the experience. At least she did not leave. I suppose that is progress.

My heart could not process what happened that day. I don't know if I ever did. I imagine a completely different conversation may have happened at that table if my heart were in its open and receptive, natural, wild state.

Deconstructing the Fortress

Today, I still wonder about the carefully designed heart fortress I built. What if I could release the wounds, the sorrows, the secrets and create a wide-open field to plant a new tomorrow? What if my heart in its wild state is the best adventure yet to come?

At about this juncture, you may hear the orchestra swelling into, "The hills are alive, with the sound of music." An epic saga about to be unleashed... . Because a wild, open heart seems like a Hollywood creation or something too fantastic to be real.

Take a moment again, right now, to open your arms wide. Feel the space around your heart. Imagine it cleared of all things stored there—the good, the bad, and the ugly. Imagine all of it being swept away to make room for new experiences.

When I do this, it feels strange, unfamiliar, both exciting and scary. I don't know what will happen next, I don't know what decision needs to be made when I am standing in a wild, wide-open field. So I just breathe into the next moment and see what arises in me. Sometimes it's a song, a string of words, the picture of a face. I listen, I discern, and then I choose to respond to the message of my heart.

What is your wild heart calling for? What is your wild heart whispering?

We can cultivate a little more wildness in our hearts, a little more natural receptiveness. We can do this by turning over the soil, by turning over the ideas we once planted. What needs to be taken out by the root? What needs to be allowed to lie fallow for a time to rejuvenate?

If you had your arms opened, you may have wanted to close them back tightly over your chest. What came up that you needed protection from? The thought, "I'm afraid," followed by whatever you imagine is a thought about the future, even if it's based on something that happened in the past? If I'm in a relationship but am afraid I will be left, I keep my heart protected. I know I am not being left right now. Similarly, if I'm afraid to speak up in my job, if I fear retaliation, I can remember I am not being retaliated against right now.

One of the things powering our fears is that we rehearse our nightmares. We don't need to rehearse our nightmares in order to somehow be prepared for them. We want to prepare for beauty, peace, love, and joy. Taking time to examine what has been planted in our hearts is a great gift we can give ourselves.

How can a wild heart heal if we don't clear it from all that's been put there unconsciously? We didn't mean to plant the idea that we were not enough. We didn't mean to plant the thought that if we don't do everything well, we won't be loved. We didn't mean to plant the fear of the unknown.

Sometimes, we allowed things to settle in and take up space because we didn't know how to stop them from taking root. We can forgive ourselves for not knowing. We can remember the wonderful Maya Angelou quote: "You did what you did, when you knew what you knew. And when you knew better, you did better." What timeless wisdom.

We start where we are. We start with our heart in its current state. We notice, we become curious, we gently excavate. We find, we release, and we replace, or we let our hearts sit fallow, waiting for a time when they feel healed enough to plant new ideas, new thoughts, new possibilities.

A wild heart is a place where love can thrive because nothing is in its way. The soil is clear of anything that chokes new growth. The soil is clear of false beliefs and self-resentment. The soil is made healthy and awaits the seeds, the sun, and the water of a new vision to blossom.

Accepting Magic
and Mystery

chapter 13

Perhaps there is a level at which we don't need to seek answers to the question, "To what end?" Perhaps there is a moment where the inquiry can end, where we can surrender to the mystery of what comes next.

There is magic to be found in allowing. The most magical things in my experiences were never, ever planned. I happened upon them. They were unplanned, but, in a way, I was prepared for magic.

I have written before about my dance with a butterfly and my greeting a cloud of thousands of dragonflies. The feeling was unforgettable, feeling my hand move and have the butterfly follow. We were communicating, communing, and life itself shimmered for me in that moment. When I was regaled by the host of dragonflies, I had just affirmed for myself that my joy and self-care were beneficial to all of life. This was an audacious affirmation, and I didn't understand why it planted itself so firmly in my mind—until the dragonflies appeared. They hovered over me, and my cells felt a vibration as if I were receiving applause.

At another time, I felt the sense of ovation from another realm when I did a moving meditation. I literally bounced on a mini trampoline, while focusing on a lit candle. I affirmed to myself something that I still find a bit embarrassing to admit. I was singing a chant to myself: "Tina, Oprah, Maya, Me. Yes!" "Tina, Oprah, Maya, Me. Yes!" After chanting this for some time, I saw a host of angels, gathered and cheering, some with what looked like tears in their eyes. The tears fell on me like glittering stars.

I called myself T.O.M.M.Y. for a while. It was my secret nickname to remind me to go for those aspects of myself that were embodied by Tina Turner, Oprah Winfrey, and Maya Angelou.

I, too, am a force, a talent, a voice, a weaver of words. I, too, have something to share that can lift and shed light. I accepted this divine assignment and have been living up to it to the best of my willingness every day since.

Then there was the occasion when I was given an assignment during a workshop to come up with my "purpose." We meditated, walked on hot coals, danced, sang, and wrote. After the opening of my heart from all the rituals, I shared this simple statement: "My purpose is to bring magic." I painted it in color with swirls and twirls of energy on a poster.

Everyone else had a purpose that explained something about what they would be doing. Mine seemed incomplete for these folks. To a person, they said, in effect, "It needs something else." Under pressure and not trusting myself I added, "Bring magic and *BE LOVE*."

I understand now that I didn't need to add anything, for two reasons. First, *no one* can question the purpose I intuit for myself. And second, bringing magic is sufficient.

I always have been fascinated with magic and anything that seems outside of linear expectations. As a child, one of my first favorite books was *Mrs. Piggle-Wiggle.* She lived in an upside-down house, and that alone was enough for me to love her. Then there was Pippi Longstocking, a girl strong enough to lift a horse, live on her own, and captain a ship. She did not doubt herself for one minute, so everything she set out to do happened.

I believed in these gospels, that you can have an upside-down house or be strong enough to lift a horse—if you declare it. It would take years for me to learn teachings that were in alignment with these ideas. It would take years to see that science had magic in it, too.

It's All Magic and Miracles

Perhaps you are familiar with a quote attributed to Einstein that declares you either see life as having no miracles, or you recognize that everything is a miracle. I don't know if he actually said this, but I like the idea of seeing everything as a miracle and in that way recognizing the magic of life.

Even if something has a scientific explanation, that alone doesn't mean it is without mystery and magic. Humankind chases the nature of life, revealing more and more every day. There is an endless realm of discovery, and therein lies the magic for me. Some like to say if something has an explanation, then it's not magic. But I say the fact that we have an explanation for how the world works at the tiniest known levels is magical, and that our minds can expand, that our capacity for love can expand—all seem magical to me.

I confess, I believe other types of magic exist, too. This is where I admit to thinking that fairies and other forms of life exist outside our view. I always use the hummingbird as my example. You can see a hummingbird and know that it has wings, although they move or vibrate so fast you can't actually see the wings. In my imagination fairies are creatures that vibrate so fast we just can't see them with our naked eyes. I imagine that someday we will be able to see them because we'll have learned how to see faster vibrations of light.

I have friends and colleagues who call themselves light-workers. They would say we are all light-workers because we are made of light. And if we could see our human form in an energetic way, we would see how much light and space is part of who we truly are.

I always found it amazing to know that an element of our bodies can be traced to stardust. This is all on the physical plane. On the metaphysical plane, even science has come to recognize an uninterrupted pattern of life—in other words, the connection between all things. Scientists have not been able to find a disconnection point. Of course, they will continue to look.

I am content with believing we are all connected, that there is no separation in Life Itself. Therefore, wherever we are, no matter how far apart, we affect each other.

It's still mysterious how water and other molecules can be affected by our emotional energy. It's still mysterious how quantum entanglement works. Contemplating these mysteries and learning, studying, and wondering are part of being on the planet. We wonder, we wander, and we discover. I think of all of this as a magical mystery tour.

What are you curious about? What do you think is magical or miraculous?

I remember reading that the egg that was fertilized to become me existed in the fetus of my mother, while she was in utero. In this way, I am connected physically to my grandmother, as she also held me in her womb. This is amazing, magical, and mysterious to me. How does that fact affect who I became? What did my grandmother experience that made an imprint on my mother in utero, that may have been coded into the egg that would become me? Some of what we carry is definitely not our own, and yet it can still show up as our experience.

I remain curious about the mystery of all that is in my cells, in my DNA from as far back as the potential of me goes. And how far back is that? I may never fully understand it, and I may never know if how I live is in alignment with my unique place in this puzzle of life. I can, however, remain curious and fascinated and accept that magic and mystery are part of it all.

The Heaven of
My Joy and Happiness

chapter 14

The concepts of heaven and hell are fraught with so much baggage, I hesitate to use the word "heaven" here. However, what I learned and understand from my experience and study is that heaven and hell are states of mind rather than places. You may wonder both about how study could illuminate these ideas and what experiences I refer to that provide any clarity.

What My Studies Taught Me

In terms of study, I offer the following. After decades of experiences in the religions of my family and friends, I began to read biblical scholars who explained that there were many writers and voices within the text of the Bible. They further demonstrated how much of what was written has been misinterpreted.

For example, the writers from different periods (since the New Testament was written over a span of decades and decades after the death of Christ) used allegories and metaphors as a regular practice, and yet some religions still interpret their writing literally. I learned about how Christian holidays were mapped to Pagan ones in efforts to replace "nature worship" with the birth, death, and resurrection of Jesus.

At Santa Clara University, during my undergraduate studies taught by Jesuits, I learned about the books of the Bible written by women. All of this, and so much more, made me curious about the source of anything I had been taught. I cannot delve into the Gnostic gospels or other "lost" scripture because that is not my expertise nor is it my purpose for writing this. But I do suggest you do your own research about the sources of anything you believe.

My Experiences

I was raised in a loose configuration of mainstream Christian religions. I was baptized in the Baptist church, because that was the religion of the godparents assigned to me. My mother did not profess any religion or share any views that I can recall in my early days. She allowed me to attend a Sunday school with Catholics while I was in elementary school because that is where my friends went. In doing so, I was exposed to Catholic dogma.

Then my mother's mother died. She was quite young, being in her late sixties. I don't know what happened to her, but I remember my mother's devastation that kept her on the couch for months.

When my grandmother's things arrived on a truck, the furniture and boxes were unloaded into our living room. My mother wept as she unpacked the glass trinkets collected from my grandmother's travels—the purple vase etched and decorated with crystals, the glass stirring sticks with delicately glass blown animals on top, heavy Waterford crystal glasses and liquor decanters. I remember the 1960s version of modern furniture being moved out, and the ornate carved wood pieces from my grandmother's San Francisco apartment being moved in.

Apparently my grandmother had abandoned her Catholic faith and had been studying with the Jehovah's Witnesses. Out of some sense of loyalty to her mother, my mother began to study them, too. This resulted in no more birthdays, Halloweens, or Christmases in our future.

In the teachings I learned in my godmother's Baptist church, I was going to a fiery hell if I did not comply with a vengeful Heavenly Father. I would only experience heaven if I accepted Jesus as my personal savior and perfectly followed his rules on Earth. Then heaven would be my destination after I die. The Catholics offered a similar instruction, except I needed to pray in a specific ways and keep the prayers up and regularly attend church to get my ticket to heaven.

This was how I understood the dogma of mainstream religions. I simplify, of course, but as a child, the explanations were simple for me.

The Jehovah's Witnesses were another flavor all together. They said there was no hell as a place. They taught that hell was death itself, with no further experience in any form. Heaven, for them, was reserved for a certain number of people, and heaven on Earth would happen for everyone after the world as we know it ends.

My following this teaching ended when I turned seventeen and left home. The final straw, for me, was the story they told about how Christ would return to the Earth and destroy everyone who had the "sign of the beast" marked on their foreheads. They explained that those who were on his side would be saved and would need to clean up all the dead bodies and mess and would be allowed to live peacefully for a thousand years. Then, the devil (who exists in their teaching) would be released from hell, to which he had been banished, and would have some time to see if he could persuade anyone to his side again. After that, paradise would reign forever.

None of this appealed to me. The idea of living peacefully for a thousand years after the massacre of nonbelievers and then still being tested again? I wanted no part of the vengeful God offered by all these religions..

My Path to New Beliefs

In my forties, I started to find people who taught a different idea. They taught that heaven and hell exist within each of us. And I remembered that, according to Luke 17:21, Christ says, "The kingdom of heaven is within you." I don't remember any mainstream religions emphasizing this, but I do remember the scripture.

The power of our minds began to be the exploration for me. What if heaven were a state of mind? And what if hell were, too?

I have certainly lived in the hell of my own mind. When I left home at seventeen and for the next twenty years, I lived with chronic depression. I was "highly functioning," but I woke up most days with a weight on my chest that never let up. I felt like I was learning to breathe in a high altitude. I did not have access to the fullness of myself, but I learned to adjust to the thin layer of air in my lungs and the timid beat of my heart.

I carried the heaviness while putting out a greater than average performance in life. On the outside, I appeared successful, healthy, and prosperous. But on the inside, I felt heavy, burdened, and sad.

The weight I carried was in the thoughts and questions I entertained every moment of every day. Was I good enough? Was I doing my children harm by being me? Did I deserve anything I was given—the money, the success, the attention? I gave my mind these questions, so it went to work. The trouble was that the source material my mind sorted through was flawed. It was based on meaning I made of my experiences as a child. I didn't have the tools to objectively look at what I stored as "real" in my mind to see if it was interpretation or fact.

I had a story in my mind that I my birth father wasn't in my life because I was somehow unworthy. I told myself that the men and boys who sexually abused me did so because

I somehow drew them to me. Since I did not know that sexuality was a healthy part of me, I hated all my desires and curiosity.

I told myself my mother did not love me because she was incapable of showing tenderness and affection. I did not understand why she did not celebrate my dark brown skin, but because she didn't, I didn't celebrate it either. I shut down my emotions when I was beaten with a belt on naked buttocks by my stepfather. I accepted that I deserved a beating for "smarting off." I accepted what I was told: that I was too much, when I was put down for being too loud or joyous or dancing in front of the TV. Through all of these instances and so many more, I created my own story of how life worked. I tucked them away and did not revisit them as an adult, but I reacted to things in my adult life from the perspective of a wounded child.

I created and maintained my own hell.

The descent into my own mind culminated in me twice swallowing pills in an attempt to give attention to my suffering and my desire for it to end. The first time, when I was seventeen, I swallowed twenty-seven Excedrin tablets, after choosing them over the blue-and-black tranquilizers I saw in the same cabinet. I was known for not being able to swallow anything without gagging and ultimately giving up. I remember distinctly looking at myself in a mirror and swallowing one pill at a time, in a precise rhythm without stopping, until I consumed the entire bottle. I then went straight to the phone to tell my sister what I had done, partly to be rescued and partly to let her know her child crawling on the floor might soon be without a babysitter. She rescued me, and the interviewing psychiatrist at the hospital saved my life by saying, "You are OK. Your mom is crazy." (My mother had told me I couldn't accept my full scholarship to the university of my choice because it was Catholic, and Jehovah's Witnesses believed they were the only ones with the truth.)

The second time, I used sleeping pills and calmly told my then-husband what I had done. He was not impressed and demanded that I get them back up and out of me—and deal with whatever I needed to deal with. Ultimately, my actions and his reactions meant the end of my marriage and the beginning of my journey into a life of loving other women.

As it turns out, I didn't want to die either time. I wanted to live a life in alignment with my heart and soul. It just took me some time to discover what that life looked like. And I continue to discover it today.

My Journey to Find Heaven

My search for heaven began as I learned to release myself from the thoughts that created hell in my mind. First, I exposed the thoughts, and then I replaced them. This was years and years of work and deliberate excavation.

This journey took me from walking on hot coals with Tony Robbins to learning the power of my own breath with Clarity Breathwork, and so much more in between.

Walking the hot coals was a demonstration of what was possible within my own mind. I always thought it was some kind of fake thing. This time, I was there. I watched the fires being built. I felt the heat, and I spent hours and days preparing my mind for the walk.

Once it was my turn, I had a power move: I had a mantra, and I was ready. There were people on either side of the coals, poised to pull me off should I lose my concentration. The person at the front of the line checked my face and body for the perfect state of readiness. I looked up at the moon, began chanting in my head, "Cool moss, cool moss."

I stepped onto the coals and walked forward, chanting at the moon, "Cool moss, cool moss." For a split second, I was aware of my feet and felt the fire. I clapped my hands in the power move I practiced, and I continued on. I saw the hands of those on the side of me reach forward, just in case I couldn't get right back "in state."

I made it!

The hoses were ready to flush my feet with water and get any small coals or embers that may have attached themselves. The sounds and people were a blur, and I remained inside my own sanctuary of self for what seemed a long time after. Once the adrenaline tapered off, I could feel a small burn between my big toe and the pad of my foot. We had been taught to use both ice and pressure on the back of our calves, which worked for me. I walked normally the rest of the night, and the next day I had no visible wound.

Fire-walking and another technique I mastered—climbing telephone polls to leap onto a trapeze—were extreme ways to release ideas that made my mind a living hell. For me, it was worth it. In those experiences, I got a glimpse of the joy and freedom that were possible.

I also got a view of potential bliss when I dove deep into the practice known as "breathwork." This gentle breathing technique is often done in community (except during Covid). It opens your emotions by gently relaxing your nervous system, entraining your own heart to a sweet rhythm of open mouth inhale and exhale. The oxygenation alone provides energy to your cells, and you have access to feeling the fullness that you are without obstruction.

We started with chanting, singing, moving, going into meditation, and then focusing solely on our breath. Sometimes the breathing itself would go for an hour. During that time, with my eyes closed, usually laying on my back, I would stop the deep breathing when I felt emotions arising.

The emotion would arise before I could identify it or what it was I was recalling. The practitioners would sense the pause and gently tap near my thalamus gland (below the neck and just above the chest.) They would whisper gently, "Keep breathing. That's it. It's safe. It's only your life force. Let whatever is emerging emerge. It is safe." With this reassurance and after having dozens of breath-work sessions, I would learn to flow with my emotions and keep breathing through them.

Tears would fall without words and without even knowing which sorrow, hurt, or wound I was acknowledging. It didn't matter. What mattered is that I was clearing some of what I was carrying and making room in my heart for the present moment, instead of stuffing it with painful experiences that I wanted to hide away.

After these sessions, I would be in a state of openness and feel like I was a blank canvass on which to create a new life. I made progress every time. Yet not unlike climbing to a vista attached to an unending elevation, I would always find more to release and more capacity for joy and bliss.

This sense of emptying out old ideas and hurts began to give me hope that a beautiful experience was available to me in this moment. This open-heart feeling was what I describe as present-moment heaven. Heaven in potentiality. Heaven in possibility. Heaven beyond thought. Heaven in full acceptance of the moment I live right now.

The Effect of Consciousness on Our Experiences

We've all heard stories about the idea of heaven, even if it is not in our belief system or that of our family. We hear about pearly gates, angels, seeing our loved ones who died. We hear about being in a better place without pain and suffering. We hear about sitting with God or Jesus and or other gods of other faiths.

My first idea of heaven came from the Christmas classic, *It's a Wonderful Life.* I wanted to believe there were a host of angels on call to help us humans navigate. I wanted a guardian angel of my own.

I didn't have any evidence of one, so I made one up by talking to myself when I was alone. I'd walk into the bathroom, look in the mirror, and say to myself, "You are wonderful, and you are going to be OK." "That was really good, what you did." "I like you." I would say the words I imagined an angel would say, and it comforted me.

As my learning and intuition expanded, I began to see *how* my thoughts had power. I began to understand that consciousness was a real thing and how, although invisible, it affected the visible. I began to cultivate my own consciousness through teachers, teachings, study, practice, meditation, yoga, and ultimately mindful eating and drinking. I began to pay attention to what I was putting into the field of my own mind and watch how it affected my experience of life. The better quality my thoughts and ideas, the better my life became. The better the quality of my consciousness, the happier and more joyful my life became.

When I learned that forgiveness was a form of freedom that freed both me and the person who wronged me in some way, I wanted my freedom more than I wanted to be right. When I understood that my perception of anything imbued it with my design and my choice, I began to chose my perceptions more carefully.

I chose to see light in every situation. I chose to look for love in every situation. I chose love over fear whenever I was capable of it.

My Experience of Heaven

The feeling and experience of heaven was present when I focused on the light and love in various situations. I did not feel heaven when I was angry, resentful, or enraged. I did not feel heaven when I was sad or guilty or confused. I didn't feel it, but I remained aware of it. Like something in your peripheral vision, you know it is there and you need only turn your attention toward it.

I felt my emotions. I raged. I grieved. I sputtered, and eventually, I turned my attention to the light and the love. It was ever present, ever available to me. I don't spend all of any day in the heaven of my own joy and happiness, but I am aware of it on most days, and I spend hours on many days breathing it in.

So perhaps this is to what end I am living: To feel and experience heaven here on earth as often as I can. To usher in an atmosphere of love and light that emanates from me when I do. And to accept myself when I cannot.

We are all, after all, doing our best in any given moment. I believe this, no matter what a person is doing. I truly mean no matter what. They are doing their best, according to their understanding, according to their capacity, according to the work that they have or have not done. Although I know everyone must experience the consequences of their actions, no human is irredeemable. Since love is ever present, every person, no matter their circumstances, can turn toward it. They can find their way to a reset button that lets them try again to experience their own heaven.

I don't claim to know if we have many lives or just this one. I hold out hope that there is more, but I intend to live as if this is it. And for me, that means doing my best with what I have, with what I know, and with what I can give.

Each day is a new possibility, a new opportunity. I intend to live.

Three Steps to Creating Your Own Internal Heaven

chapter 15

What if we are here to experience heaven on Earth and to share the joy that emanates from our alignment with heaven right here on Earth? So many questions arise when we contemplate this idea.

For example, you may wonder about selfishness versus self-lessness. My experience is that the more generous we are, the more joy we feel. In the United States, where I was raised, greed is a disease, and so is overwork. People seek more, better, bigger, greater, and find no peace when they achieve level after level. Instead, they live in chronic disappointment about not achieving bigger, better, greater, and more.

If we were to apply the idea of bigger, better, greater, and more to love, kindness, and tenderness, we could shift the balance of the entire human experience. What if every single person were here to be more love, greater love, deeper love? I can imagine this world. Can you?

I started writing this book because I wondered if I needed to love deeper or wider. I now understand that this is a false choice. The expression of love is boundless, and it flows in all directions. So if I chose to focus my love on my mate or my close family and I love them with a fierceness and wildness in my heart, holding nothing back, this is as powerful as any demonstration of love that can exist, as long as I don't close my heart to anyone else I encounter.

That is to say, it is not better, bigger to love more people. Our expression of love benefits everyone, whether we know them or not. Acting as love with an open heart is sufficient to being a loving presence with whomever you encounter. I don't think we need to go find people to love. I think we find the love inside ourselves and apply it liberally to every person and situation we encounter.

It may seem a strange example to insert here, but this came immediately to mind: the young woman who painstakingly recorded the death of George Floyd on her phone. She acted as love in that situation to the best of her ability and imagination. It turns out that her action inspired an entire movement, an awakening to be triggered in millions around the world.

It was love that made the life that was being taken worthwhile. It was love that witnessed the one who killed without being aware of his connection with the brother under his knee. It was love for justice, fairness, kindness, and goodness that inspired people to action, to find a solution to the root cause of feeling separate from each other.

Love applied is a reason to live.

Three Actions to Create a New World

We always wonder what one person can do in this big wide world, so full of contradiction, confusion, and seeming chaos. One person creating their own internal heaven matters to the whole. Each of us can *rise, heal,* and *create* a new Earth right where we are.

Rise. To rise is to lift our attention to a higher view of ourselves and our lives. Hovering above ourselves and observing who we are and how we are in life is a first step.

We are not simply the one who was born, had experiences —whether tragic and/or blissful—and then arrived at this moment. We are the ones who observe, who are aware, who know we are more than our bodies and our physical senses.

Rise up, and truly look at yourself. See how you are part of something larger than what you call "your" life. See how you are part of Life Itself. See the magic and mystery of your existence in the intricate patterns of nature, humankind, and the cosmos. See that you are a part of it all.

In this way, we recognize our place in the unfolding all around us. We are integral. We have a note to add to the harmony. We have a word to add to the prayer. We have a movement to add to the dance.

Heal. The beauty of our bodies is that they have inherent intelligence and the resources to heal themselves. If we keep them functioning with good food, water, and limited stress, they can do an amazing job of keeping us well.

Even when illness or disease occurs, the body's natural healing mechanisms can reverse conditions. This is a lot of what pharmaceuticals are trying to do—communicate with the body and give it a boost in doing what it already is capable of doing. Sometimes medical and pharmacological treatments just deal with superficial symptoms rather than triggering true healing. But those treatments can give the body enough rest to trigger its own healing.

The body is miraculous in this way. We don't need to tell it to heal a wound. When wounded, it automatically begins sending white blood cells to ultimately repair what has been damaged or broken.

Our minds can heal, too. Our emotions can heal. Our souls can heal. The difference is that we are our own medicine. Our words, our thoughts, and our behaviors toward ourselves and the disruptive situation determine our recovery.

For example, many of us may need to heal from experiences with our family of origin. We have to decide to do so within ourselves. We cannot wait or expect our parents or siblings to repair any wounds we think they contributed to creating. We have to be willing to face what hurt, forgive all who took part, including ourselves, and relieve our minds, emotions, and spirits of the burden.

Family of origin is a tricky thing. Some people have great family experiences and remain close to each other all their lives. Some, like my family, break up and move away from each other at majority age and never truly reconvene. In our case, my siblings and I came back together for our mother's memorial, but hadn't been all together for decades before. There were so many secrets and lies. We never bonded; we survived. Still to this day, we make efforts to check in, to show care. Every one of us is past fifty now, and our wisdom is emerging and a gentler love is emerging. We are healing, each in our own way.

Do what is necessary to heal what still causes you pain. In this way, what you create can be from new ideas rather than forged from the past.

Create. Create what is yours to contribute to the world around you. I often hear people say, "I'm not creative. I don't have a creative bone in my body." This is simply not true. We are creative beings because we have thought. Your thoughts are creative because they are a field of energy and you bring to them what you routinely think and say.

You create experiences every day, determined by where you put your focus. This is so simple, and it's not easy. You wake up and declare, "This is a new day. This is a good day." And I guarantee you, it is. We only lose faith when what we consider *good* doesn't happen. But if we look deep enough, we will find the good.

I have stated to myself that I am ready to be used for the good of all, and may I find joy in it. Sometimes the thing I am called to do is not what I hoped would call me, but in the end I find the joy in it. In my case, I get new callings to create all the time.

Every few months, there is something I want to contribute. It could involve music, writing, performances, service, learning, teaching, or playing. I don't know one day to the next what is mine to create. But I have begun to trust. Somedays, my contribution will be baking cookies, or staying in my PJs, or working on a book or a class.

I have learned to accept whatever it is I create as a gift to myself and others, and I'm working on not judging the value. Dancer and choreographer Martha Graham's words ring in my mind always: "It is not your business to determine how good it is. ... It is your business to keep it yours, clearly and directly, to keep the channel open... ."

Such wise words. Keep the channel open. Keep your heart open. Keep your mind open. Open your mind to the greater aspect of yourself. Continue to grow. Continue to create, and never mind to what end. Embrace the questions and journey on.

appendix

The following Daily Guides originally appeared in the June 2023 *Guide for Spiritual Living: Science of Mind* magazine. Some reflect June dates, such as Loving Day, Father's Day, and Juneteenth, but the meanings they convey are appropriate any day.

As in the rest of this book, I interchangeably used the words God, Infinite Mind, Source, the All-Good, Divine Intelligence, the Presence, the Divine Pattern and Life, all of which refer to that which created and creates, by whatever name you call it.

My inspiration for these Daily Guides is an expression I learned from reading Emma Curtis Hopkins. "If you know what Life, sweet and free, looks like … claim for yourself a sweet, free life." We must include ourselves in tender, loving care to contribute our best to life. One of the ways I care for myself is with music and lyrics; you'll find some of my favorites here. I hope these guides will help you toward your version of life, sweet and free and overflowing with love.

DAY 1 — Going Out Of My Head

Goin' out of my head, over you, out of my head over you, out of my head, day and night, night and day and night.
~ Little Anthony and The Imperials,
Goin' Out of My Head

Our body is not separate from that infinite Intelligence that created it. ~ *Ernest Holmes,* A New Design for Living, *p. 45.3*

As a child, I relished the times when I could take out my favorite 45, put it on the tiny record player, and let it blare through our playroom walls. As the song by Little Anthony and The Imperials, "Going Out of My Head," played, I would run back and forth across the room and throw myself into the pillows of the couches on either side. I sometimes played the song three or four times until (even at five years old) I was exhausted. I loved the feeling of moving my body and the exhilaration of sweat and a rapid pulse.

Almost sixty years later, I must remind myself to get out of my head and revel in moving my body. There is a freedom in my body that I often cannot access in my mind. Our teaching relies heavily on our relationship to the mind, consciousness, and thought. To live a joyful life, I have found that my body needs my care, attention, and respect.

As Ernest Holmes reminds us, our bodies are one with Infinite Intelligence and are included in our spiritual practices. I love to remind myself of those first words in an oft-repeated prayer or affirmation: "I live and *move* and have my being in God." As students of Science Of Mind, we would do well to get out of our heads and into our bodies through movement.

AFFIRMATION: Today, I move and relish the gift of my body and let my mind rest. It is safe to get out of my head.

DAY 2 — Breathe Again

If love ends, I promise you; I promise you that I shall never breathe again.   ~ *Toni Braxton,* Breathe Again

Love is the eternal flame of the Universe, nay the very fire itself.   ~ *Ernest Holmes,* The Science of Mind, *p. 478.3*

Love songs tend to be dramatic. In the above excerpt from "Breathe Again," made famous by Toni Braxton in the early 1990s, the singer promises to stop breathing if the love from another ever ends.

Holding our breath is something we do when we are afraid—afraid of loss, fearful of the unknown, or simply anxious about daily life. We need never fear the absence of love. We can know that another person can never limit the love available to us. Principle teaches us that love is everlasting, ever present, fueling the Universe. We can remind ourselves of the gift of life, of Spirit, within us with every breath we take.

When we take our breath for granted, we withhold its deep cleansing power. We sometimes stay in the shallow part of our lungs and don't give breath to our body's fullness. Do you notice when you breathe? Take a moment right now and breathe deeply. Let the rise and fall of your chest remind you that you are alive now.

Since we know Love as Spirit never ends, we can breathe deeply into that understanding. Breath work is a beautiful form of tenderness and caring for ourselves. Deep connected breaths access our inner life, opening and releasing whatever blocks our joy. Yogic breathing, meditative breath, alternate nostril breathing—play with it. Try it all. Breathe in the Love that gave life to you.

AFFIRMATION: Today, I breathe joyfully and effortlessly, knowing that eternal Love breathes Itself as me.

DAY 3 — Free Your Voice and Sing

I sing because I'm happy, I sing because I'm free. ... Glory Halle-lujah, you're the reason why I sing.
> ~ *Gregory L Gilpin*, Why We Sing

We know by intuition that there is something beyond what we have so far consciously experienced.... Poets have sung of it.
> ~ *Ernest Holmes*, The Science of Mind, *p. 465.2*

"You're the reason why I sing," I whispered to her when we finally met. I waited in a long line in 1996 to meet Dr. Maya Angelou. I told my friends standing with me, "I don't know what to say!" The love, reverence, and awe I felt in her presence seemed to leave me without words.

So when I arrived, greeted by her wide-open smile, I began to sing, "I sing because I'm happy," and she joined in. "I sing because I'm free. Glory Hallelujah," we sang together. I leaned in and said, "You are the reason why I sing." As it turns out, that particular song was among Dr. Angelou's favorites, and she sang it all the time.

Sometimes we need to sing. We need to let the expression of our souls come through the melody, the notes, the pace, the volume. People often say, "I can't sing," or, "I'm not a singer." We need to be more tender with ourselves. We were all given a voice. We don't need to compare ourselves to anyone else. We don't need to do it right or in tune. We just need to sing.

Science supports what singing does for your well-being. It lowers stress, boosts immunity, improves mental health, and can help you cope with physical or emotional pain. Singing needs to be part of your toolbox in caring for you.

Find a place. Free your voice. Sing.

AFFIRMATION: I use my unique voice to sing a song of praise and wonder. I let my soul express. I am free of judgment and lean into joy.

DAY 4 — The Wonder of Touch

See me, feel me, touch me, heal me.
> ~ *The Who, See Me, Feel Me*

There is no need to feel that one should forego any beneficial pleasure or joy in living.   ~ *Ernest Holmes,*
A New Design for Living, *p. 59.2*

The wonder of touch is something I forget. With our social distance training over the past few years, we all forget. Sometimes I absent-mindedly run my fingers over my hair, squeeze a tired neck, or hold a perfectly cold orange in my hand without noticing.

If I pay attention, this sensational gift of touch is a powerful tool for my self-care. We tenderly care for plants, animals, and other people, especially babies. We intuitively know that touch is healing and expresses love. Even so, we often forget to apply it to ourselves. We forget to ask for what we need. We forget to indulge in massages or pedicures, if our life and preferences allow the time and expense.

On the other hand, it costs nothing to lay on the grass or float in water, letting blades tickle or water caress. My mate's primary love language is touch. We took the test from the book called *The Five Love Languages* by Gary Chapman. Since I know this about her, I reach for her hand and touch her back when we are sitting near because these are the "words" she can hear that fill her heart.

Touch is also emotional. Do we let ourselves be touched by what we see, hear, or feel? What about the simplest things, like touching another with a smile or receiving the touch of another's gaze? We are energetic beings, and our energetic signature writes itself in every encounter.

AFFIRMATION: Today, I am willing to give and receive touch. I give through smiles, loving gazes, and hands-on love, too.

DAY 5 — Intimate with The Infinite

Let me be intimate with the Infinite, let me be deeply revealed.
~ Amy Steinberg, Intimate with the Infinite

We long for and need a conscious union with the Infinite. This is as necessary to the nature and intellect of man as food is to the well-being of is physical body.   *~ Ernest Holmes,*
The Science of Mind, *p. 153.1*

In my book *Radical Self-Tenderness*, I write about practices to cultivate tenderness in ourselves. I write about yoga, breath work, massage, singing, dancing, music, tapping, and more. The central tenet from which all the others derive is our relationship with Spirit, with the unseen inner light and fire.

Intimacy with other humans requires a sense of trust and vulnerability. Intimacy with Spirit or the Infinite requires our knowing. We have to know that God is Love Itself. We have to know that Infinite Mind casts no judgment. We have to know that we are always welcome and always safe.

Our intimacy with the Infinite comes with constant awakening, prayer, and practicing of the Presence. The more we drop into the inner chamber of our hearts to commune with the God Self, the more such intimacy becomes our default position. Holmes reminds us that our relationship with the Source of Life is as necessary as food. We feed our bodies, and our relationship with that which created us feeds our souls.

As Holmes said, when we are intimate with the Infinite, in conscious union with It, we have all we need for an abundant and light-filled life. This intimacy is our ultimate self-tenderness—a deep, gorgeous surrender in God.

AFFIRMATION: Today, I welcome true intimacy with the Infinite. I let myself be revealed as the expression of God that I am.

DAY 6 — When I Love Myself

When I love myself, just the way I am, I reveal my power wherever I am, and anytime I can redefine, get a new paradigm, and let myself grow. ~ *Andy Anderson,* When I Love Myself

Self-condemnation is always destructive and should never be indulged in by anyone. ~ *Ernest Holmes,*
The Science of Mind, *p. 465.4*

Condemnation means expressing extreme disapproval. Do we sometimes think we deserve that? What if I disapprove of how I handled that, disapprove of my weight, disapprove of my unhealthy habit, disapprove of my failings?

We believe our disapproval of ourselves will result in change. Instead, we find that our self-condemnation results in stagnation and fear, even despair. I appreciate how strongly Holmes advocates against this practice as one that "should never be indulged in by anyone." He doesn't say you shouldn't atone for errors, apologize, or make amends. He admonishes you not to condemn yourself. Instead, we can love ourselves as we are now and love ourselves into our evolving expression.

We are made of Love. And the more we dwell in the love for ourselves and others, the more we call forth a loving presence as our way of being. In Andy Anderson's song, he reminds us that at any time, we can redesign, get a new paradigm, and let ourselves grow.

May each of us accept ourselves and love what is. May we each let love transform all the seemingly broken places. And let us return to the wholeness that is the truth of who and what we are—pure Love.

AFFIRMATION: Today, I love myself just the way I am, and Love loves me back.

DAY 7 — What You Believe

I believe in kindness/I believe in simple things/I believe in the preciousness of all beings/I believe in tomorrow/Despite the troubles we face/Because I believe in the human race

~ Erika Luckett, Kindness

The Law operates on our beliefs—as we believe them, not as we hope them to be, but as we actually believe them to be.

~ Ernest Holmes, How to Use the Science of Mind, *p. 89.1*

When I began understanding the power of my mind and my thinking patterns, I paid closer attention. I started eliminating the sad songs I repeatedly sang and replaced them with songs that expressed hope and possibility.

We all have a soundtrack in our minds, full of expressions, catchy phrases, ideas, and beliefs. We are taught what to believe about money, success, goodness, evil, right and wrong, and, most significantly, what to believe about ourselves. My upbringing taught me more about what not to do than who to be. "Don't be greedy; don't be conceited; don't be lazy, mean, or too smart for your britches." It took a lifetime to learn to believe in my inherent worth and goodness.

When I accepted that I was made of Divine Substance and emanated as a unique expression of the Divine's idea, I felt a quickening in my heart that has never left me. I remember the day after I left my corporate work. I wasn't sure how I would define myself and how I would be recognized. I placed my hand on a tree near a creek where I walked, and I heard these words: "I recognize you." A sense of peace descended, and I leaned into the embrace of something greater.

What do you believe about yourself? Tenderly explore, inquire, and let your knowing unfold.

AFFIRMATION: I am willing to take inventory of my beliefs, and I lovingly release anything that no longer serves the highest good for myself and others.

DAY 8 — The Errors of Ignorance

No mistakes have been made in God. All the ways that we seem to fail in God all fade; it all fades into God.
> ~ *Rickie Byars*, All Fades Into God

Our ignorance and lack of understanding are the only sources of our undesirable conditions and situations.
> ~ *Ernest Holmes*, A New Design for Living, *p. 35*

Being wrong is what I call my "big wound." From my experience in life, I decided being wrong was the worst thing that could happen. And in so doing, I caused myself all manner of pain. When I lived for decades with the thought that I needed to get an A+ from the world in everything I did, I was living in ignorance. I was living in ignorance of the perfect Pattern within me that was never wrong.

Instead of being wrong, I was learning. I was gaining understanding. The consequences I received were information, not punishment. In the world of form, I witnessed and experienced the consequence of my own or others' actions as if they were the law of my life. When I learned that the law of life was Love, or Spirit, and put my focus on that, I began to see that my mistakes were in fact my own ignorance of my true nature.

Everything I have done to this point was my best, according to my understanding. I now move more and more as the Love I am.

When we truly know ourselves as individualized expressions of God, we are led to the right action. We care for ourselves in a tender way when we remember we are learning every day.

AFFIRMATION: I revel in being a student of life. As I learn and grow, more and more the Love that is Spirit moves through me. I give myself an A+ for all my lessons.

DAY 9 — Food for Your Body Feeds Your Spirit

Every day for suppertime, she'd go down by the truck patch and pick her a mess of poke salad and carry it down in a tote sack.
                              ~ *Tony Joe White*, Poke Salad Annie

Food must be a spiritual idea; there is an intelligence within us that will guide us to a proper diet.
                    ~ *Ernest Holmes*, The Science of Mind, *p. 259.2*

In addition to our mental diet, which is primarily under our control, our physical diet also reflects the choices we make. We may have people around us who espouse ideas that do not align with our highest and best, but we don't have to agree with them, mentally or physically. We may live in a place surrounded by foods that are not life giving, but we don't have to ingest them. Even if we have limited types of food available, we still have choices.

There are as many theories about food as there are people to espouse them. I've found only a few agreements in it all: Drink plenty of clean water, eat plenty of leafy greens and other vegetables, and, as author Michael Pollan so eloquently said, "Eat food, not too much, mostly plants."

With all the confusing information, fads, advertising, and the big food industry vying for our attention, the most tender thing we can do is follow Holmes's advice and see food as a spiritual idea. If we meditate on our wholeness and if we pray affirmatively that our cells express their purpose, we can choose food and drink that align with these ideas.

Each of us is an individuation of God. Our personalities, practices, and even food will be unique to us. And all things we study, learn, and experiment with will change as our understanding grows. *Buon appetito!*

AFFIRMATION: I am divinely guided in all things, including my food choices. I give myself the grace to learn, grow, and change in divine order.

DAY 10 — Shed Your Tears

Can't hold back my tears, that would be a crime, cause I look pretty cryin'.   ~ *Lizzo*, Exactly How I Feel

Infinite presence becomes personalized at the center of your being—warm, colorful, loving, and joyous.
                    ~ *Ernest Holmes*, A New Design for Living, *p. 201.5*

Reading the above words from Holmes, I wonder: Do tears have a place in my personalization of the Presence? Are tears part of our being "warm, colorful, loving, and joyous"?

I would love to give myself the gift of tears. I have a mistaken belief that only a few things are worthy of or reserved for crying. Death, loss, hurt, or pain. Since I assiduously avoid all of those, I avoid crying. That is not to say I haven't shed tears for those I love who have died or been hurt. Rather, I allow myself a few moments and then shake it off.

In some ways, I'm waiting for something terrible enough to unload the decades of grief that I've stored up. When another race-related murder happens, when war breaks out, the Earth is damaged, natural disasters devastate, or children are in any way harmed, I feel a stab of sadness and transition, and then I almost immediately transition to rage or action. The few times I really let the tears fall, I found incredible peace afterward. In a way, my tears cleared the illusion of anything I created in my mind that seemed to not be God, to not be Love.

Tears are a gift. Sorrow is a gift. I'm coming to understand that the colorful aspect of the Presence individualized as me is all of my emotions, fully felt. The full range of my human experience reveals that at the end of sorrow, at the end of tears, what is left is the essence of Life: Love, Itself.

AFFIRMATION: Starting today, I give myself permission to explore and fully experience the tenderness of my tears.

DAY 11 — Rest, Knowing the Source of Your Energy

I am tired; I am weak; I am worn; through the storm, through the night, lead me on to the light.
> ~ *Thomas A. Dorsey*, Precious Lord

Perfect trust in God within is the secret of relaxation, rest, and renewal. ~ *Ernest Holmes*, The Science of Mind, *p.257.1*

I've always loved the spiritual "Precious Lord." It was the first thing I sang publicly to embrace my African American heritage and find my voice. Over the decades since the song was penned in 1932, it has had many meanings for those who sing it as a prayer, a declaration of faith, or an appreciation of the eternal Presence and home in God. I sing it as a reminder: "Precious Lord, take my hand, lead me on, help me stand." In it, I recognize the ever-present Law operating as Love, and I accept its embrace.

I am sometimes weary, tired, and feeling worn. This is part of the human experience. We express life through the lens of a body that requires attention, care, and rest. Even as we know the unlimited nature of Love as Life flows through us, there are times when we do not allow it free rein. We worry. We struggle. We forget. And we find ourselves tired.

When we rest, we have the opportunity to remember the source of our energy and aliveness. When we rest, we have the capacity to learn, grow, and practice the Presence more and more. At my current level of understanding, I accept the limitations of an earthly body, and therefore it becomes my law and my experience.

I am tender with my body and rest when I feel tired. I refine my thoughts when I feel weary, and I let God energy rejuvenate any worn places.

AFFIRMATION: Today, I rest and renew my aliveness by trusting God as the Source of all.

DAY 12 — National Loving Day

Love is all you need.   *~ The Beatles*, All You Need Is Love

Does the thing I wish to do express more Life, more happiness and more peace to myself and, at the same time, harm no one?
~ Ernest Holmes, The Science of Mind, *p. 70.2*

June 12 is National Loving Day. On this date in 1958, Mildred and Richard Loving married. Richard was labeled "White," and Mildred was labeled "Black." Officials in Caroline County, Virginia, gave them a choice: go to jail or leave their home in Virginia. They fought back, and eventually, the United States Supreme Court, in 1967, struck down laws against what was then called "interracial marriage."

The world is full of limiting ideas. We can choose to accept or abide by them or express our lives in alignment with our own values. We can live as Holmes advocates, according to what brings more Life, more happiness, and more peace to ourselves, while not harming anyone else.

The Lovings contributed to a greater possibility for millions of people. In today's world, some folks struggle with how others express their gender, how they identify their gender, and who they love. It appears that the world has a limited idea of love that doesn't include everyone in it.

We have the privilege and opportunity to expand and include everyone, knowing that every person, without exception, is an individualized expression of God. To be in a world that works for everyone, we must start by having a foundation of peace. Finding our own peace and allowing others to do the same, we harm no one. By finding and expressing love and allowing others to do the same, we harm no one.

AFFIRMATION: Today, I choose my partner and my purpose, declaring it good and very good. May it be so for all beings everywhere.

DAY 13 — I Accept What Is

Don't go changing to try and please me, ... I love you just the way you are.   ~ *Billy Joel,* Just the Way You Are

My body is the body of God, the Living Spirit Almighty.
                    ~ *Ernest Holmes,* The Science of Mind, *p. 261.2*

When my wife and I went on our first safari on the African continent, we spoke about how amazed we were at the variety of plants, trees, grasses, flowers, birds, and, of course, all the wild beasts of the Serengeti. There was an endless display of multiplicity in the unity of nature.

All of life breathes the same air, warmed by the same sun, yet all of life distinct. Even when we saw a dazzle of zebras, when we looked closely, each individual stood out on its own. Human beings share this amazing diversity, and yet we sometimes resist and labor toward a more uniform look, especially when it comes to our amazing bodies. We are bombarded with images of the perfect male or female form. No space for gender-nonconforming or transgender people or anyone outside the norm in most of the mass media.

Each of us, as we are in any given moment, is a unique expression of Life. We can be more love in the world by honoring, caring for, and tending to the miracle we move around in on this Earth. That includes accepting ourselves in our many renditions. The one who looked back at us in the mirror at seven is the same one looking back at seventeen or seventy. Our bodies are a manifestation of what we have experienced. We can accept it all and continue to evolve.

AFFIRMATION: Today, I accept and approve of myself, including my body, just as it is.

DAY 14 — Easy to Love

I am not my hair; I am not this skin. I am the soul that lives within.
~ India Arie, I Am Not My Hair

Actually, we seek to discover our real self, that which is back of what we appear to be. *~ Ernest Holmes,*
A New Design for Living, *p. 3.4*

A poet friend of mine once did a reading in which she said, "You are so easy to love." She repeated it over and over, and I noticed people in the audience beginning to cry.

We can sometimes be so hard on ourselves. I know I can. I go over all the things I haven't done right, the things I haven't done at all. I criticize my doing and being. I look in the mirror and wonder if I'm lovable as I am.

I am deeply grateful for the lessons in Science of Mind, Unity and other New Thought teachings because they have helped me recognize the truth of my being. I am not my outward appearance. I am not my accomplishments. I am not my progeny and their accomplishments. I am not my possessions or my bank account. I am not my social circle or social followers.

Instead, I am an individualized expression of the One Life, which is God, and my divine essence is the perfect pattern of that which created me. This is also why I am grateful for practices like meditation and prayer. Deep within, when I am still and quiet, I am flooded with understanding, and I know myself to be one with the All Good. With this understanding, I can agree with my poet friend, Mara Glatzel, "You are so easy to love." And so are you, and so are we all when we look past the presentation and see the Presence within.

AFFIRMATION: Today, I see and know my true self, and I declare with joy, "You are so easy to love."

DAY 15 — Strengthen Your Spiritual Muscles

I didn't know my own strength, and I crashed down, and I tumbled, but I did not crumble; I didn't know my own strength.
> ~ *Whitney Houston*, I Didn't Know My Own Strength

Today we hear much about this power and the way to develop it, for as yet, we express one in part, being unaware of the whole.
> ~ *Ernest Holmes*, The Science of Mind,
> *e-version p. 421*

A scriptural mantra I embraced for a while was, "If God is my strength, whom shall I fear?" I would repeat this in moments when I felt afraid. Usually, the fear was based in my mind about not measuring up in some way. It wasn't fear of losing a job, shelter, or access to food. It wasn't fear for my physical safety. It was fear created by my identification with who I thought myself to be.

The type of fear I experienced doesn't require strength; it requires right contemplation. It requires seeing the truth in ourselves as unique and wonderful expressions of life. When we see rightly, our fear is released, and we lean on our true identity as God.

In our human experience, we need to build strength. Strength is required to have the resilience needed to navigate life on this planet. We need strong faith, strong, consistent spiritual practices, and strong inner centers.

While I do the work to build muscle, I know my mental, emotional, and spiritual strengths are perhaps more important. Even if my body diminishes in power over time, there is a power in me that never diminishes. This power lies in knowing I am centered in God, flowing from God, moving in God.

AFFIRMATION: With God, in God, as God, I am strong in Spirit, and the world cannot harm me.

DAY 16 — Create Space for Yourself

Going back to Saturn, where the rings all glow, rainbows, moon-beams, and orange snow, on Saturn, people live to be two hundred and five.   *~ Stevie Wonder,* Saturn

Space is the distance between two specific forms—the cosmic world.   *~ Ernest Holmes,* The Science of Mind, *p. 633.4*

I have a T-shirt given to me by one of our children, a fellow introvert. It has the NASA logo and the words, "I need my space." I love the play on words because I know that to take care of myself, I need both inner and outer space.

I used to be fond of singing the Steve Wonder song "Saturn," describing a place where people are at peace, experience order, and live long and healthy lives. In the past, life on this planet sometimes seemed unbearable, so I fantasized about another place. I've since grown in understanding that I have unlimited space within me, and I have the privilege of creating space in my outer world.

I create space when I say the magic word: No. No to invitations, no to activities, no to giving more than I have at the moment. I create space with solitude and solitary walks. I create both inner and outer space sitting in meditation. I have found space listening to music, especially in Portuguese, a language I don't understand but feel.

Do you know how to create space for yourself? What do you need? Asking and answering these questions is part of loving and caring for yourself. It's unlikely that we will be able to visit another planet, but even if we did, we'd bring our consciousness with us. Create space within, for as within, so without.

AFFIRMATION: Today, I allow myself the space I need. I cultivate the peace within.

DAY 17 — Let Intuition Be Your Guide

Guide my feet while I run this race, guide my feet while I run this race, for I don't want to run this race in vain.
                    ~ *African American spiritual,* Guide My Feet

There is an intuition within you that already knows you are one with Good. ... It is the voice of God in you.
                    ~ *Ernest Holmes,* This Thing Called You, *p. 29.4*

One of the most liberating things I can do for myself is to let my intuition or inner sense guide me. In doing so, I am not controlled by the opinions and noise of the world but instead am guided by Infinite Mind. The noise of the world is constant and often lacks wisdom.

If you believe, as I do, that Infinite Mind leads us to Itself and It is All Good, then you know, as I do, that we can trust our inner voice, cultivated by dwelling on God. When we lean into the Presence within us, we give ourselves a great gift. This is the ultimate in self-tenderness—giving total trust and total surrender in God.

When we think we have to figure everything out, that we have to know in advance every step of our journey, we become prisoners to our plans.

Intuitive messages guide my feet if I tune inward. The Divine Pattern reveals Itself in our experience when we expect and accept It. My greatest joys come when I am aware that God is my source, substance, and supply. I did not create myself or the miracle of birth that I have experienced and continue to experience. I did not create the alchemy that happens when God's creations interact.

I just follow the whispers and try desperately to stay out of the way of what Ralph Waldo Emerson called "the Divine Circuits."

AFFIRMATION: I am guided by my inner voice, tuned to the Infinite Mind. All wisdom is mine.

DAY 18 — Father's Day, Your Way

Don't go and talk about my father, 'cause God is my friend, Jesus is my friend. He made this world for us to live in and gave us everything, and all he asks of us, I know, is we give each other love. ~ *Marvin Gaye*, God Is My Friend

Your endeavor, then, is not so much to find God as it is to realize His Presence and to understand that this Presence is always with you. ~ *Ernest Holmes*, This Thing Called You, *p. 160.2*

Holidays and observances differ for many of us—because of our histories, our culture, our religious or nonreligious beliefs, and our state of mind. Some folks find no meaning in any holidays or observances, and some a specific few. Some look forward to every reason to celebrate, and some are awash in longing or memories.

Father's Day is intended to honor fatherhood. What if you didn't have a father in your life? What if you long to be a father? What if your father was someone you feared rather than celebrated?

Every day that is called out for a specific purpose is an invitation to reflect, consider and/or celebrate. None of these approaches is a requirement. We have the opportunity to make any day our own.

I lived some of my life without a father figure and all of my life without my genetic father. I choose to celebrate Father's Day by being thankful that my absent father created a longing in me that led to my rich spiritual life. The unconditional love I imagined he could provide became the unlimited responsiveness of the Infinite's embrace.

Whatever this day means to you, it has value. This is the richness of our human experience.

AFFIRMATION: Whatever this day or any day means to you, honor it and make space for your fellow humans who experience it differently than you do.

DAY 19 — Every Day Is Freedom Day

Your first name is Free; your last name is Dom because you still believe in where you are from.   ~ Pharrell Williams, Freedom

So humans must be created with the possibility of limitless freedom and let alone to discover themselves.
~ Ernest Holmes, The Science of Mind, *p. 109.3*

On June 19, 1865, freedom from slavery was proclaimed in the state of Texas, the last holdout in a post-Civil War United States. This was two years after President Abraham Lincoln issued the Emancipation Proclamation, changing the legal status of approximately 3.5 million enslaved Africans and their descendants.

Most enslaved people were not present at the reading of the Emancipation Proclamation. And those who received the word may have had different reactions. We can imagine whoops and hollers from those prepared to grab a small sack of personal goods and hit the road. Some were willing to head out to an unknown but free future. Some may have hung back from celebrating, unsure what to do. And others may have begun immediately executing a plan they had been nurturing within.

But in Texas, folks continued working for their enslavers without knowing there was freedom afoot.

What has always fascinated me is that this tardy holiday is recognized as Freedom Day for all African Americans, even though it originated in Texas. It took a while for me to see the wisdom of it. I know see that Freedom Day was not declared until everyone had the word, until everyone was set free. There is also wisdom in knowing that if we rely on the world, our freedom can be delayed.

AFFIRMATION: Today, I recognize, celebrate, and initiate my freedom to be. I share the news of freedom now.

DAY 20 — Accept Joy

You've done what no one thought could be; you've brought some joy inside my tears.   ~ Stevie Wonder, Joy Inside My Tears

I am surrounded with friendship, love, and beauty. Enthusiasm, joy, vitality, and inspiration are in everything I do.
~ Ernest Holmes, A New Design for Living, *p. 236.4*

I was reading literature from The Movement for Black Lives and was thrilled to see this statement: "Joy is a form of resistance." The idea is that any system, person, or institution that practices oppression is thwarted when we choose our own joy.

We can react to all the "isms" and injustices of the world with our tears and our actions and, at the same time, remain whole inside. This wholeness inside brings a sense of joy to the surface of our lives, knowing that no matter what comes our way, there is that which is omnipresent, omniscient, and omnipotent within us.

Joy as evidence of gratitude is an idea that always has worked for me. Whenever I'm not expressing joy over an extended period of time, it's because I have forgotten where to focus my attention. My prosperous and adventure-filled life includes so much for which I am grateful. I noticed over the years that as I switched my focus on all that I have versus anything I believed lacking, lack fell away.

Joy comes from our inner well-being. No one or no thing can take it from us. We may experience lapses of feeling it or remembering that it is there. And we can activate our joy on demand by putting our focus on the changeless Divine Pattern inside each of us.

Tenderly, tenderly we let our wellspring of joy flow.

AFFIRMATION: Today, I remember my joy. I release any resistance to its free flow in my life.

DAY 21 — Pray Without Ceasing

The moment I wake up, before I put on my makeup, I say a little prayer for you.   ~ *Dionne Warwick*, I Say a Little Prayer

Whatever process of reasoning you go through to convince yourself of Divine Perfection is of no particular importance. It is a realization of this Perfection that heals.
   ~ *Ernest Holmes*, How to Use the Science of Mind, *p. 21.3*

Having a practice of prayer makes my life work. I don't reserve prayer for when something is or is not happening. I pray to remember who I am, every day.

Prayer is like a spiritual savings account. The consciousness you develop or accumulate is there to draw on at any time. I appreciate the expression, "Pray without ceasing." In today's world, we need to live in a constant awareness of love and in a constant prayer of love. I pray while walking, doing dishes, looking at sunsets, and bathing my body.

I use spiritual mind treatments in my prayers by starting with the recognition of God as the All Sufficiency, knowing I am one with It, declaring my good is at hand, and being grateful in advance that it is already done. The formula of prayer is not where the power lies. The power lies in the practice and in the feeling of unity we experience.

In addition to prayer, when I am focused on knowing the truth, I meditate. In meditation, I listen and let my heart speak. I don't try to clear my mind; I let go of trying. In meditation, I rest from making an effort. Each day, I spend a few minutes just noticing my aliveness; this is meditation and medication for my soul. Prayer and meditation are like the cycle of breathing—inhaling and exhaling.

I receive. I know. I release and let go.

AFFIRMATION: I pray without ceasing and I know everything I need is right where I am. Prayer is a gift I give to myself.

DAY 22 — We're In This Together

Help, I need somebody. Help, not just anybody. Help, you know I need someone. Help. ~ *The Beatles,* Help!

We not only wish to help people, we should have an equal desire to teach them how to help themselves. ~ *Ernest Holmes,* How to Use the Science of Mind, *p. 42.4*

When is the right time to ask for help? Depending on what we were taught, we have different ways to answer this question. Some families work together as a way to get things done; some divide up chores. Some of us watched an overburdened parent handle the household or a beleaguered parent work too much outside the home without rest.

In school, we are taught, "Keep your eyes on your own paper. Do your own work." Where do we learn to cooperate and include? I worked as a high-tech executive into the early 2000s. My career flourished because of the help I received. I did what I knew how to do and showed up as my best because others did the rest.

Now I try to remember to ask for help before I feel overwhelmed. I try to anticipate what I need and engage folks with me. It's not always easy to ask, but it gets easier with practice. When I include others and ask for help, I also give people a chance to connect with me and to model asking for help for themselves.

We are all in this together. The more we help each other, the further we can go toward a world that works for everyone, a more loving and just world where everyone is included. When we try to do it all ourselves, we miss building relationships and sharing the accomplishment with others.

AFFIRMATION: Today, I am willing to ask for help. Even if in small ways or with small things, I contribute to the circulation of good in the world.

DAY 23 — Celebrate You

*I'm marching on to the beat I drum. I'm not scared to be seen.
I make no apologies. This is me.*   ~ *Keala Settle and
The Greatest Showman Ensemble,* This Is Me

*Originality means exactly what the word signifies—something
unique, different, unlike anything else that ever was or ever
shall be.*   ~ *Ernest Holmes,*
How To Use the Science of Mind, *p. 74.2*

All the self-help books on the planet (including mine) tell
us that our own self-regard matters. We hear it over and over
because it is a powerful principle. The messages repeat: "Love
your neighbor as yourself." "What we give, we are; what we
give, we receive."

When we withhold from ourselves, we lose our supple-
ness, our capacity to receive. On the other hand, when we
give ourselves sweet kindnesses and words of affirmation,
we create the fluidity to give and receive.

You and I are one of a kind. If we let that sink in, let the
miracle of our existence sink in, we can invite celebration.
Every day that we wake up or have an opportunity to experience our unique selves, we should celebrate and not take
it for granted.

I generally make a fuss about my birthday. It's not about
gifts but about acknowledging that I am here. Are you willing
to celebrate the one and only you, on your birthday or any
other day you choose? What if we created an event that said
to those in our lives, "Here I am. I want you to know me. Here
is my favorite reading, art, music, and activity." Why wait for
folks to try to create this in honor of your life once you are
gone? What if we celebrate now?

AFFIRMATION: I am willing to find ways to specifically celebrate that I am here.

DAY 24 — Permission to Play

When you get the choice to sit it out or dance, I hope you'll dance.
                              ~ Lee Ann Womack, I Hope You'll Dance

Just as children enter into play or into a game, ... there is a light-heartedness, a delight, a sense of fun, sheer exuberance in the joy of living. ~ Ernest Holmes, A New Design for Living, *p. 206.3*

I love to play games. I especially like spelling games or dominoes—silly, easy games that make me smile in relaxation or bring out a laugh. I like to play in childlike ways. For example, I painted a wall in our garage with renditions of trees, flowers, and rainbows. I will sit at the beach and color in a journal, making shapes or mandalas.

Another way I play is to dance. When I'm alone, I'll put on a favorite jam and move around the room in whatever way feels good to me. I tend to stay in my head a lot, so playfully moving my body is enlivening and shakes loose some of my seriousness.

In our Science of Mind teachings, we can get caught up in focusing on thinking, thinking, thinking. Fun gives our minds a rest and lets the Greater Mind find an opening to impart some beautiful insights and wisdom.

When do you give yourself permission to play? To be silly? Do you ever have a thought to do or say something, and then your inner critic pipes in with, "That is ridiculous! No, you will not wear a tutu to the beach. No, you will not put on your Halloween costume in December." Why not? Some of us think to be spiritual, we must be serious, predictable people whose every action is on purpose. Not in my understanding. Our teaching could move even further and faster if we were more playful.

AFFIRMATION: Today, I accept my silliness and let myself play in whatever way comes to mind.

DAY 25 — Find Your Laughter

Let the children's laughter remind us how we used to be.
                    ~ *Whitney Houston*, The Greatest Love

We need have no feeling of solemnity, no sense of dealing with heavy and ponderous ideas or laborious work to be done.
                    ~ *Ernest Holmes*, A New Design for Living, *p. 206.3*

In the spirit of yesterday's ideas about play, laughter is another way we give our hearts delight. A delighted heart is an open channel for all the good that can flow into everyone in its path. Just as I don't cry enough, the same could be said for laughing. I smile a lot, and I appreciate the sweetness of that, but there are deep belly laughs in me that want to come out more often.

My wife, Jane, loves to tell the story of how I sometimes let a belly laugh rip when we are on a plane. I'll be watching one of the movies I can count on to tickle me, and I'll laugh loudly without realizing how much I'm being heard throughout the plane. She never quiets me down because it brings her such joy, and we've both decided that others being disturbed by laughter is an OK thing.

Laughter truly is a medicine. Science has documented the health benefits of good guffaws. Just now, Jane called me from the beach, saying, "Come to the balcony and take a picture of me down here so I can take a picture of you up there." She cracks me up. This is good. Laughter is good for us.

Find things that make you laugh, no matter how goofy. Imagine the field of sadness, grief, and despair being disturbed by your laughter, and let it rip.

AFFIRMATION: Today, I find reasons and ways to laugh out loud. It is a tonic I can never take too much of, and I welcome it.

DAY 26 — Dolce Fa Niente

That's why I'm easy. I'm easy like Sunday morning. Why I'm easy, easy like Sunday morning. ~ *Lionel Richie,* Easy

Everyone is an incarnation of eternity, a manifestation in the finite of that infinite that Emerson tells us "lies stretched in smiling repose." ~ *Ernest Holmes,* The Science of Mind, *p. 388.1*

Dolce fa niente is Italian for the "sweetness of doing nothing." When I first got together with my mate, I introduced the idea of a day of nothingness. "What is that?" she asked. "Truly, we do nothing," I said. "No agenda, accomplishments, checklists, just flow with the day and see what our hearts call for." She was amazed at how giving herself this freedom would create space for clarity and joy.

Sometimes we need to take a break from doing. If you are like me, you have a pretty endless list of things to do that you can choose from any given day. If you are gainfully employed, the list is not always in your control. If you work for yourself or are retired, you can decide more easily when to indulge in *dolce fa niente.*

I especially appreciate the word, *dolce,* which means sweetness. Doing nothing can awaken the sweetness from within. We are made of the substance of God, the substance of Love, not just the emotion but the force—that which acts through us and as us.

Activate your love center by doing nothing. All your to-do lists will be there when you return to them, refreshed, clearer, and more in tune with your natural self. Nature teaches us the four seasons: repose, germination, growth, release. We regularly need to let the soil rest, let the mind rest, and let ourselves experience the sweetness of doing nothing.

AFFIRMATION: Today, I care for myself by enjoying a day of nothingness.

DAY 27 — Your Presence Is Enough

It's a new dawn, It's a new day, It's a new life for me. And I'm feeling good.   *~ Nina Simone,* Feeling Good

Feel your pulse; it is consistent and harmonious. How many times do you breathe in a minute? The human skeleton? Superb! Perfect adaptation of structure to purpose.
                    ~ Ernest Holmes, A New Design for Living, *p. 8.4*

Suzanne Scurlock wrote a book called *Full Body Presence.* I recently joined one of her online workshops because I benefited greatly from her book years before. In the workshop, she helped us tap into the wisdom of our bodies.

I loved being fascinated and curious about what my hips might tell about my willingness to swing through life. I appreciated my shoulders for letting me know what I was carrying that was not mine. Tapping into the wisdom of my body was exhilarating in every part, inside and out.

The greatest wisdom I received was looking into the knowledge from my organs, especially the front and back of my heart. What was I sending out, and what was I receiving? I noticed my heart was often above its resting rate at night. What was it saying?

Being fully present in my body, I began to listen more generously to its messages. Now I hear the whisper from my heart, kidneys, and lungs, telling me, "Gentle, gentle, dear one. You are worthy of rest and sweet care. Your presence alone is enough."

As you scan your own body, do you notice areas you've not paid attention to? How do those feel? What messages do they have for you? Perhaps the next check-up we need is the one we do ourselves.

AFFIRMATION: Today, I bless every part of my body. I praise its function, and I gain its wisdom.

DAY 28 — Remember, in Celebration and Release

Memories, like the corners of my mind, misty watercolor memories of the way we were. ~ Barbra Streisand, The Way We Were

My affairs are in the hands of Him who guides the planets in their course, and who causes the sun to shine. Divine understanding attends me on the way.   *~ Ernest Holmes,*
The Science of Mind, p. 522.4

The only gift my mate wants each Christmas is a photo book I make of our lives. I try to capture the highlights from thousands of pictures of people, places, and things. I have found that the most important and potent memories are the people. Taking time to remember gives us time to reflect and deepen our gratitude.

Memories are not always picture-book perfect. I have memories of errors I made in the past or at least things I think I'd do differently now. This is where remembering gives me a chance to work on forgiveness. When I scan my heart and find a stuck place, I know there is an opportunity to clear it. I am motivated to do so, and thereby I allow more love to flow through an unobstructed channel.

I give myself the gift of remembering for two main reasons: first, to breathe in with gratitude all that has been experienced, and, second, to transform my memories that have hardened. For gratitude, I love to share memories with others, whether sitting with a photo book in my lap or looking at a sweet video. For the scars that may be in the way of my open heart, I usually tend them in solitude. I take the time I need to feel, remember, release, and revel in the sweetness of an even more open heart.

AFFIRMATION: Today, I give myself permission to remember in celebration and in release.

DAY 29 — Rejoice and Be Blessed

If anyone should ever write my life story, for whatever reason there might be, you'll be there between each line of pain and glory 'cause you're the best thing that's ever happened to me.
~ *Gladys Knight,* Best Thing that Ever Happened to Me

We begin with a child's sense of discovery, which enables us to be ready to accept the new and marvelous world we will encounter. ~ *Ernest Holmes,* A New Design for Living, *p. 4.3*

On June 29 in the late 1970s, I was a nineteen-year-old giving birth to twin children. I experienced preeclampsia and nearly died in the recovery room from a seizure. I woke up with my breasts bound full of milk, thrashing about, crying out, "Where are my babies?" My daughter was born three minutes after her brother, and his exit caused a cord to get tangled around her neck. My last memory was of the doctor reaching inside me to pull her out.

For a long while after I gave birth, I lived in survival mode. Getting from one feeding to the next, getting through their first two years and finding myself a single parent for a while at age twenty-one. Those years were so full that I could not rejoice in the blessing their lives were to mine.

Sometimes it takes space to breathe before you recognize the miracle that has happened, Those children, conceived on an eighteen-year-old's honeymoon, made me. How brilliant is Divine Intelligence to immediately give me people through which to experience and develop love? I could not be consumed with myself. I needed to care for them, so I learned to give.

I made countless mistakes, but I became a better version of myself under their gaze and sweet embrace. I am forever blessed by their presence in my life.

AFFIRMATION: Rejoice, knowing everything happens for you, and it's even better than what you can imagine.

DAY 30 — Release, Let Go, Be Free

I release and I let go. I let the Spirit run my life, and my heart is open wide. ~ *Rickie Byars,* I Release and I Let Go

The Law of God operating within establishes that which is good, beautiful, and true. It is done. I accept. I believe. I know.
~ *Ernest Holmes,* How to Use the Science of Mind, *p. 36.1*

Whatever is in the way of your inner peace, let it go. Let it go. Remember those chalkboard exercises of yesteryear? I could write the above statement one hundred times to let it sink in.

Whatever is in the way of your inner peace, let it go. I've been practicing letting go for years and continue to discover what it means. I've gone to extremes to let things go: walking across of hot coals to release my fears of living full out, flying on a trapeze to recognize my inherent ability to soar.

Nowadays, I may choose to take a pilgrimage, as I did to Alabama to let go of my rage over the history of racial terror in our country. I was so devastated by emotion that I had to lay in bed and heal through tears. And then I got up and walked across the Edmund Pettus Bridge, facing my fears and finding my freedom.

Sometimes letting go can be much simpler, nothing that requires a pilgrimage or a circus act. Always, it requires a willing and open heart. I appreciate the exercise of untethering my soul. I often sit with the *samskara,* little wounds I find circulating in my heart, taking up space where love could flow. I open my arms wide, feel the feeling—even when it seems excruciating—and let it pass through.

In what ways do you let go? Don't you love the feeling of freedom you receive? Don't you want more?

AFFIRMATION: Today, I release, and I let go and let Spirit run my life.

DAY 31 — Choose Hope

Just when I thought our chance had passed, you go and save the best for last.   ~ *Vanessa Williams,* Save the Best for Last

Hang on, it ain't gonna be long, stand tall, walk through walk on, be still, hand over your will, give up control, let it be, let it go, hope.
~ *Amy Steinberg,* Hope

I used to think of hope as something weak. I thought to myself, "Why hope? Why not know and do and make it happen?" I now realize there is beauty in hope, just as there is beauty in all of our emotions.

This is the juice of being human. We can feel in complex and comprehensive ways. We are not just reptilian creatures, with flight/fight/freeze as our options. Amidst any situation, any sorrow, fear, or rage, we can choose to hope. We can choose to imagine another possibility. We can choose to look for the light in the dark.

I've listened to the Amy Steinberg song *Hope* dozens of times. I sometimes need to remember to "hang on" and "stand tall" because, as she says, "You're going to make it in the end, my friend."

I watched the film about Diana Nyad, the marathon swimmer. She tried and failed five times before making a historic sea swim that included sharks, jellyfish, fierce weather, and unquenchable waves. Her crew was battered but maintained the tiniest hope that she could pull it off. That hope and her fierceness proved enough to make the dream come true.

Hope is real. It is an emotion that can move me forward, no matter the outer circumstances. Some moments it's all that I have. And this is OK.

AFFIRMATION: Today, I chose hope and let the possibility of good move me to the next moment, where I can chose again.

About the Author

Rev. Christie Hardwick is best known as a leadership development advisor who coaches with a spiritual lens. She advises clients and organizations in the for-profit and not-for-profit sectors to get to core issues that enable value-centered work and leadership. After twenty years as an executive in the high-tech industry, Christie became an ordained minister with Centers for Spiritual Living.

Combining her passion for spiritual principle, music, and spoken word, she founded Inspiration Gatherings and produced uplifting events on Cape Cod with some of New Thoughts' most prolific musicians. After publication of her first book, *Radical Self-Tenderness*, she continues to be a sought-after workshop leader and speaker online and nationwide.

She enjoys four children and seven grandchildren with her wife, Jane. They live between Walnut Creek, California, their home base as they travel the United States in their RV, and Umbertide, Italy.

You can follow her on Facebook or take classes and hear her speak through soulcallglobal.org or illli.org.

Made in United States
Orlando, FL
07 December 2024